PRAISE

TELLING THI

What an effective one-two punch. Luis brings the seasoned wisdom
of one of history's most effective evangelists. Tim is one of today's
best organizers and trainers of evangelism leaders. *Telling the Story* is
a wonderfully helpful book for those in the field of evangelism
and for those just launching out.

LON ALLISON
DIRECTOR, BILLY GRAHAM CENTER
WHEATON COLLEGE

Luis Palau is an extraordinary man for extraordinary times.
His perspective about evangelism is cutting edge, revolutionary and
relevant. It reminds one of the brand of evangelism that Jesus spoke
of. Isn't that a notion in this day and time! Anyone who reads this
book should be prepared to turn the world upside down.

SUZETTE CALDWELL
ASSOCIATE PASTOR, WINDSOR VILLAGE UNITED METHODIST CHURCH
BOARD CHAIR AND PRESIDENT, KINGDOM BUILDERS' PRAYER INSTITUTE

Luis Palau will go down in Church history as one of the truly great
evangelists of our time. The Lord has mightily used him to reach
millions through his numerous crusades worldwide and through his
new and creative approaches to evangelism in recent years. *Telling the
Story* will not only change your perspective on evangelism,
but will also change your life. I highly recommend it.

PASTOR DAVE GIBSON
PASTOR OF MISSIONS AND EVANGELISM
GRACE CHURCH, MINNEAPOLIS, MINNESOTA

Filled with practical advice and sound biblical teaching, *Telling the
Story* is a must-have resource for every evangelist. Luis Palau
and Tim Robnett offer the wisdom that can only be gained
through years of experience.

JOSH McDOWELL
CHRISTIAN APOLOGIST
EVANGELIST AND AUTHOR, *EVIDENCE THAT DEMANDS A VERDICT*

When backpacking, an adventurer insists on having every life-saving essential in his pack. In evangelism, this book *is* the pack!

MIKE SILVA
EVANGELIST, PASTOR AND MISSIONARY

The message of Jesus never changes; the messenger does. Luis Palau and Tim Robnett have written a wonderfully insightful book based on real-life experience. If you have ever wondered if you have the gift of evangelism, this book will help you discern it. If you *know* that you have the gift, this book will inspire and drive you.

BRAD STINE
AMERICA'S COMEDIAN

Enough beating around the bush about evangelism! Luis and Tim bring a fresh, straight-to-the-point approach to this critical subject—answering tough questions with direct and compelling insights that are a joy to read and a challenge to the believer's heart.

WAYNE WATSON
SINGER/SONGWRITER

Ready to reignite your passion for reaching this generation with the good news? Luis Palau and Tim Robnett have delivered the most practical and biblical book on the calling, gifting and life of the evangelist that I've ever read. I only wish that *Telling the Story* was available when I started in evangelism!

JOSE ZAYAS
TEEN EVANGELISM DIRECTOR, FOCUS ON THE FAMILY
EVANGELIST AND AUTHOR, *AIRBORNE*

TELLING THE
STORY

LUIS PALAU
TIMOTHY ROBNETT

Regal

From Gospel Light
Ventura, California, U.S.A.

Regal

PUBLISHED BY REGAL BOOKS
FROM GOSPEL LIGHT
VENTURA, CALIFORNIA, U.S.A.
PRINTED IN THE U.S.A.

Regal Books is a ministry of Gospel Light, a Christian publisher dedicated to serving the local church. We believe God's vision for Gospel Light is to provide church leaders with biblical, user-friendly materials that will help them evangelize, disciple and minister to children, youth and families.

It is our prayer that this Regal book will help you discover biblical truth for your own life and help you meet the needs of others. May God richly bless you.

For a free catalog of resources from Regal Books/Gospel Light, please call your Christian supplier or contact us at 1-800-4-GOSPEL *or* www.regalbooks.com.

All Scripture quotations, unless otherwise indicated, are taken from the *Holy Bible, New International Version*®. Copyright © 1973, 1978, 1984 by International Bible Society. Used by permission of Zondervan Publishing House. All rights reserved.

Other versions used are
NASB—Scripture taken from the *New American Standard Bible,* © 1960, 1962, 1963, 1968, 1971, 1972, 1973, 1975, 1977, 1995 by The Lockman Foundation. Used by permission.
NCV—Scriptures quoted from *The Holy Bible, New Century Version,* copyright © 1987, 1988, 1991 by Word Publishing, Nashville, Tennessee. Used by permission.
NKJV—Scripture taken from the *New King James Version*. Copyright © 1979, 1980, 1982 by Thomas Nelson, Inc. Used by permission. All rights reserved.
NLT—Scripture quotations marked (*NLT*) are taken from the *Holy Bible, New Living Translation,* copyright © 1996. Used by permission of Tyndale House Publishers, Inc., Wheaton, Illinois 60189. All rights reserved.

© 2006 Luis Palau and Timothy Robnett
All rights reserved.

Library of Congress Cataloging-in-Publication Data
Palau, Luis, 1934-
   Telling the story / Luis Palau, Timothy Robnett.
      p. cm.
   Includes bibliographical references.
   ISBN 0-8307-3900-9 (trade paper)
   1. Witness bearing (Christianity) 2. Evangelistic work. I. Robnett, Timothy, 1950- II. Title.
   BV4520.P24 2006
   248'.5—dc22   2006020250

1   2   3   4   5   6   7   8   9   10   /   10   09   08   07   06

Rights for publishing this book in other languages are contracted by Gospel Light Worldwide, the international nonprofit ministry of Gospel Light. Gospel Light Worldwide also provides publishing and technical assistance to international publishers dedicated to producing Sunday School and Vacation Bible School curricula and books in the languages of the world. For additional information, visit www.gospellightworldwide.org; write to Gospel Light Worldwide, P.O. Box 3875, Ventura, CA 93006; or send an e-mail to info@gospellightworldwide.org.

DEDICATION

To those called of God to proclaim the good news of Jesus Christ to your generation, we dedicate these writings. Yours is a noble call with many challenges, roadblocks and special rewards. As Paul the apostle said to the Colossian church, "I, Paul, have been appointed as God's servant to proclaim it [the good news]" (1:23, *NLT*). May the words of these pages bring refreshment to your spirit and determination to your soul that you will faithfully, lovingly and with great boldness announce that Jesus Christ offers the gift of eternal life without charge. May you determine to serve Him with passion and patience. May you find in His Word the message that never changes. And may you find on your knees before Him the method that will capture your generation.

CONTENTS

Acknowledgments

To the Luis Palau Team—thank you for your partnership through 40-plus years of ministering the good news of Jesus Christ. Your great love for Jesus and your sacrifices in service for Him have largely been untold, yet only with your dedication and devotion have we seen such wonderful results through the years. Much of what we write is because of a team and not just individual gifting or work. So to any and all who have been members of the Luis Palau Association, we pray that this work brings some sense of appreciation for your years of labor in the harvest for our Lord.

FOREWORD

A word fitly spoken is like apples of gold in settings of silver.
PROVERBS 25:11, NKJV

All of us have experienced the reality of this proverb. We cannot put a price tag on the value of hearing the right message at just the right time. As we listen to a timeless truth "fitly spoken," it elicits that "Aha! I'm not crazy!" response that sets us back on course.

That's what Luis Palau has done in *Telling the Story* for every soul that has taken the Great Commission of Jesus Christ seriously. From the subtle and unidentifiable characteristics that make up the personality and calling of an evangelist to the broader questions of function and relevance, Dr. Palau has tackled this topic from the vantage point of one who has not just studied the matter theoretically but also lived it out practically. More than seven decades of sharing Christ has earned this man of faith the title of "evangelist." His true-life illustrations have a dimension of understanding and knowledge that are not found through hypothetical theories of research but gleaned only from in-the-trench faith.

You might be tempted to bypass this book because you don't consider yourself an evangelist. I would caution you not to make that decision too quickly. Coauthor Timothy Robnett adds his years of experience in the pulpit to his passion for evangelism and brings us a multifaceted view that causes us to look at the world and the Church in a way that will draw us into the heart of the Great Commission as more than mere spectators. And whether we ever step foot outside our own small realm of influence, we will have a greater impact in our world because of the insights we have gained through the inspiring and energizing call within the pages of this book to spread the good news of the gospel.

In my position as senior pastor at Calvary Chapel Ft. Lauderdale, I have had the privilege over the last 20 years to witness the faithfulness of God in responding to my own call to share the good news. Although our church has grown from four people to a number beyond my own human ability to muster (which bespeaks the handiwork of God), I can't help but wonder how much more encouraged I would have been in the journey had I received these "apples of gold" back when the enemy was telling me I was crazy to even think that I could ever make a difference for Christ.

You may never stand before thousands of faces in a crowd as Luis Palau so faithfully does, but you will stand before someone who needs to hear the good news of the gospel. The time you invest in reading this book can make the difference as to whether you are encouraged and equipped for the job with the inexplicable sense that you are just a simple tool in the hand of a Mighty God.

Bob Coy
Senior Pastor, Calvary Chapel
Ft. Lauderdale, Florida

PREFACE

What if you knew that God wanted you to help proclaim the life-changing gospel of Jesus Christ? Where would you turn for guidance?

Bruce (not his real name) always had a dynamic, extroverted personality and passion for preaching salvation. Even as an undergraduate student, he knew his calling in life—God wanted him to follow in the footsteps of mass evangelists like Billy Graham to bring the good news of Jesus Christ to thousands of people. But when Bruce approached the president of his Bible college for career guidance, he received less than encouraging advice. "Mass evangelism is a thing of the past," said the president. "Focus instead on serving the local church."

Confused but undaunted, Bruce began that journey. For many years, he served in pastoral positions, often feeling frustrated and underutilized. He was faithful to his work with the church, but deep in his heart, Bruce knew there was more that the Lord wanted him to do.

In 1996, Bruce connected with Kevin Palau, executive vice president of the Luis Palau Evangelistic Association, at a crucial moment in the organization's history. The Palau Association had a vision to support and prepare the next generation of evangelists, and as one of the first Next Generation Alliance partner evangelists, Bruce launched the full-scale evangelistic ministry he had dreamed about since college. Now, Bruce serves the Church as an itinerant evangelist, bringing the gospel message to thousands of unsaved people around the world.

From itinerant preachers to international missionaries, untold numbers of people like Bruce have heard the call to evangelism but struggle to hear anything further to help them move forward. *Where do I begin?* they wonder. *How do I start an evangelistic ministry?*

Telling the Story is designed to help you with those questions and give you the tools to reach your world through evangelism.

GUARDIANS OF THE GOSPEL

TIMOTHY ROBNETT

Only one person holds the title of "evangelist" in the New Testament—"Philip the evangelist" (Acts 21:8)—and he was an outlaw.

In Acts 5, Peter and the other apostles were told in no uncertain terms to cease and desist their work. But their desire did not wane, and the men continued to minister. After a stint in the city slammer—and a miraculous jailbreak—the apostles were brought before the highest court.

"We gave you strict orders not to teach," the judge told them. "Yet you have filled Jerusalem with your teaching." The response was not what his honor expected to hear.

"We must obey God rather than men!" cried Peter. "The God of our fathers raised Jesus from the dead—whom you had killed by hanging Him on a tree. God exalted Him to His own right hand as Savior that He might give repentance and forgiveness of sins to Israel. We are witnesses of these things, and so is the Holy Spirit, whom God has given to those who obey Him."

One can only imagine the fury that erupted in the courtroom. How dare Peter and his fellow apostles blatantly defy the law? Cries rang out for the death penalty.

One man saved the apostles from death. Gamaliel, a Pharisee, spoke in their defense. "Leave these men alone! Let them go!" he urged the court. "For if their purpose or activity is of human origin, it will fail. But if it is from God, you will not be able to stop these men—you will only find yourselves fighting against God."

The apostles were flogged, warned once again to refrain from speaking in the name of Jesus, and then released. But nothing could keep these good men down. In fact, so much work was still to be done that the apostles decided to bring seven more employees on board. And so Philip became a fellow outlaw.

From Samaria to Caesarea, Philip never stopped preaching the gospel, performing miracles in front of large crowds, and teaching the Bible to searching souls. Although the Bible does not specifically detail all that Philip accomplished, Acts 8 covers the highlights. Philip's life can instruct us in the purpose of evangelism and the role of the evangelist.

WHAT IS EVANGELISM?

Evangelism is sharing the good news of Jesus Christ through word and deed, through preaching and living, and through telling and showing. Followers of Jesus are witnesses of their faith in Christ as Savior and Lord (see John 15—16). A "witness" is one who tells what he or she has seen and heard.

You do not have to ask grandparents what they think about their grandchildren—they will tell you. They do not have to be coaxed into showing pictures of their grandchildren. It comes naturally. In the same way, our witness is as natural as our breathing. We are daily witnesses of what controls our passions. It is inescapable.

As believers, we should be daily witnesses of our faith and the good news upon which our faith is founded. What exactly is the good news? The biblical content centers unquestionably around the person and work of Jesus Christ—He is the good news. His salvation work makes it possible for the Holy Trinity to commune with those who, by faith, receive the gift of eternal life. There are consequences—immediate and eternal—for those who turn away from this good news.

The good news of Jesus Christ deals with the ultimate issue—physical death. What a powerful message is found in the resurrection of Jesus Christ and all who believe in Him! Resurrection power conquers sin and death, and by faith one is justified (see Rom. 3:21-24; Heb. 11:6).

The gospel is a message of hope about a relationship that connects people with a saving God who has done for them what they cannot do for themselves. The good news is all about a relationship once destroyed but now restored. The Bible calls this "eternal life" (see John 17:3-4) and a relationship that comes as a gift from God (see Eph. 2:8-9), and it transforms our human experience by the presence of God within us (see Col. 3:1-4).

In Christ, we are made children of God (see John 1:12; Heb. 2:11). This relationship is possible because God the Son paid the redemption price—His death for our sin. His life was given for us, and our lives are lived because of Him (see 1 John 2:2; 2 Cor. 5:21; 1 Pet. 2:24). Now the Spirit of God can indwell us, living within and through us to impart grace and truth so that others can see Christ in us, the hope of glory (see Col. 1:27-28).

The message of this good news is God's power made available to all who hear, bringing God's deliverance to them. God's power comes through the gospel of Christ. Therefore, the Church is called to preach Christ, crucified and raised from the dead! Sharing this good news with those who are without Christ is the essence of evangelism.

WHO IS AN EVANGELIST?

Evangelists are God's gift to the Church to empower and mobilize her mission of announcing the good news of Jesus Christ. Yet many in the Church have shunned evangelists for a variety of reasons and have dropped the term "evangelist" for other, more acceptable, terms.

Today, we have church planters, church growth experts, communicators, missionaries, musical artists . . . but dare we say evangelists? There are a few like Billy Graham, Luis Palau, Greg Laurie and Franklin Graham who are well known. But it seems that we have reserved this biblical term for only a fraction of the many God-gifted evangelists given to the Church for the purpose of winning the lost and equipping and motivating the Church in the ministry of evangelism.

Yes, evangelistic methodologies need to change and address the culture in a contemporary way. Yes, evangelists, like pastors, give the gospel and the Church a black eye from time to time. But the Church does not need to abandon the term nor those whom God has given to the Church as evangelists. What does it mean for a football team to play a game without a running back? What would it be for a basketball team to play without a key shooting forward? The team may play the game, but not very successfully.

The Church needs to realign itself with biblical teaching. We need to seek God and identify those given by Him for the purpose of spiritual harvest. We need to position those harvesters for effective ministry with, through and for the Church. We need to identify, train and position these gifted ones from God for the purposes He has given them.

Evangelists equip the Church in strategic methodologies for winning the lost to Christ. They exhibit a unique creativity and keen insight as to how to win people to Christ. They promote boldness within the Body of Christ to reach out to those who need Jesus as Savior and Lord. They inspire new ideas, new ways and new approaches for presenting the gospel to each generation. They are on the cutting edge of culture and have unique insight into the changes in culture, often serving as the bridge between the Church and the world.

Are all evangelists the same? It is a popular view to believe that all evangelists are sanguine personalities who love people, love the spotlight, talk continuously, meet people easily and seem to be natural communicators. Often, these personality types do make great evangelists. But the real question to ask concerning who is a called and gifted evangelist has to do with how the Spirit of God uses that person over a lifetime of ministry. Is the major impact of that individual's life winning the lost or equipping the Church to win the lost?

Ephesians 4:11-12 indicates that all evangelists are given to equip the saints for the work of the ministry. Along with a reaping ministry, evangelists are used by the Spirit of Jesus to prepare the Church in its witness for Christ, giving information, illustration and inspiration.

There are, however, a broad array of evangelists and evangelistic styles. Some evangelists are effective communicators through their preaching, writing and use of mass media. Some are used of God to support the work of evangelism with their gifts of administration, personal work, resource development and management. Although an evangelist, D. L. Moody spent a significant amount of his time and energy the last 20 years of his life raising funds and starting four schools to train workers in evangelism.

The question to ask yourself is whether the Spirit of God is using you to bring in the harvest. If the answer is yes, to whatever degree, then you are part of the evangelistic work.

Many are called to work with the evangelist or an evangelistic ministry in strategic and fruitful roles. Cliff Barrows serves along with Billy Graham. Phil Comer, Dave Luben and other musicians serve alongside Luis Palau. Music evangelists such as Jeff Moore equip the Church for evangelistic ministry and effective preaching of the gospel in their music-oriented ministry. Youth With A Mission uses multiple musicians, actors and power teams to present the gospel in a variety of ways as they preach Christ worldwide. God has given to the Church many who have a calling for evangelism, many who are anointed evangelists, and many who are workers in evangelism. As the Church accepts, affirms and supports this host of workers ministering for the Church, we will see the Church grow in historic proportions.

God has given pastors who do the work of evangelism (see 2 Tim. 4), all believers as witnesses (see John 15–16; Acts 1:8) and many as workers (Matt. 9:37-38), along with the host of workers to whom the Lord Jesus Christ also assigns areas of specific ministry in evangelism (see 1 Cor. 12:4-7). Believers are not only gifted by the Holy Spirit but also given specific ministries in which to use those gifts. Evangelists then have a significant workforce to lead and to equip for ministry.

For example, some are called to evangelize children, such as Mark Thompson and Christian Holtz, who are part of the Next Generation Alliance, or those who serve with Child Evangelism Fellowship. These men are evangelists who have a unique passion and effectiveness in reaching children for Christ. Other ministries such as Youth for Christ, Young Life and Intervarsity Christian Fellowship focus on reaching the youth (13 to 21 years of age). Many who identify with these ministries have a special assignment from the Lord to work with the younger generations. Some are called to work in the recovery movement, chaplaincy ministry or the military. So along with gifting, one needs to identify and focus on the specific areas of ministry. For some, such as Luis Palau, the field of service is the whole world.

Evangelists are the "sales force" for the good news. This worldly metaphor may carry some negative baggage, but in fact, that is how God uses evangelists. They communicate clearly and convincingly that Jesus is the way, the truth and the life. They help those without Christ confront their need for the Savior and embrace the One who can deliver them from themselves. Evangelists who love the Church will serve the Church as reapers in the harvest.

AM I CALLED TO BE AN EVANGELIST?

Do you feel that you're an evangelist? What do other people say? (Do not listen only to close friends and relatives.) Where is the fruit of your ministry? Are people coming to Christ? Are people going on with Christ as committed disciples? These are sobering questions.

To be an evangelist worthy of the Cross, one must live a righteous life. This is not to say that any of us are perfect or that we preach a message of condemnation. This is to say we are marvelously saved by the wonderful love of God through Jesus Christ and that we are different because of that good news. We have a high and holy calling, which calls for our utter dependence on the Spirit of Christ within to guide, empower, correct and use us for His glory. Let none of us quickly say, "I am an evangelist sent by Jesus Christ." Let the fruit of our ministry show that God has chosen us.

Evangelists who will be guardians of the gospel in the twenty-first century must walk in holiness before Jesus Christ. The Church cannot afford to promote, affirm or support in any way those who do not live and serve with integrity. But the issue is not a one-way street. How will the Church know whom to support and minister if there is no relationship with the evangelists? How will the evangelists in the twenty-first century have credentials and credibility if there is no interaction with the Church? In what ways is the Church actively identifying, training, affirming, utilizing and supporting gifted evangelists?

To understand if you are called and gifted as an evangelist to serve the Church in ministry, there are several essential questions you must answer: Do you have a desire to minister as an evangelist? Does your passion consistently burn for winning people to Christ? Do you seek out the lost? Are you excited about speaking, preaching or praying for the lost?

Do you see people coming to Christ through your ministry? Does the Spirit of God use you as a reaper of the harvest? As you interact with people, do they come closer to a commitment to Jesus Christ?

Do others in the Church say you have this gifting? Do Church leaders affirm your gifting and call you an evangelist? Do others seek your counsel and mentoring in reference to evangelism? Are you asked to lead in the area of evangelism in the context of your Church or sphere of influence?

Some theologians, Church leaders and pastors question the value and role of the evangelist today. Just recently, a prominent seminary president responded to my question concerning the role of the evangelist in the twenty-first century with these words: "I believe the pastor fulfills the role of the evangelist today." For some, today only pastors and teachers are operative leaders for the Church. Yet the Bible and history clearly demonstrate the vital role of the evangelist. I believe evangelists have a strategic and irreplaceable work with, through and for the Church.

Frequently, students raise the question, "What do I have to do to become an evangelist in the twenty-first century?" As the director of the Next Generation Alliance, it is exciting to know that many Christians today are concerned and committed to sharing the good news of Jesus Christ. Because God is a God of love and relationship, He desires to make Himself known to people. He wants to connect with those He has created in a personal way, and He uses His chosen children to be the instruments of this communication. So today, in ever growing numbers, I believe the Spirit of Jesus is raising up a whole new generation of evangelists to share the transforming message of the good news of Jesus Christ.

Are you called to be part of sharing that message? This book will assist you in answering key questions as to how to become an evangelist in the twenty-first century. It is our hope that it will empower you to begin fulfilling God's call to proclaim the gospel!

CHAPTER 1

THE HEART OF THE MATTER

CHARACTERISTICS OF A GREAT EVANGELIST

LUIS PALAU

"Why him?" More than a few people asked that question during D. L. Moody's evangelistic campaigns in the 1870s throughout Great Britain. Thousands upon thousands were coming to faith in Jesus Christ, and cities were beginning to sing the praises of God. The impact of the gospel was astonishing.

Yet Moody himself was considered anything but extraordinary. His education was limited. His speech was unimpressive. His messages were short and simple. Nevertheless, everywhere Moody preached, hundreds publicly came forward to confess the Lord Jesus as their savior.

In Birmingham, England, one theologian went so far as to tell Moody, "The work is most plainly from God, for I can see no relation between yourself and what you have done." Moody laughed and replied, "I should be very sorry if it were otherwise."

Thousands of evangelists proclaimed the gospel throughout the world during the closing centuries of the last millennium, but looking back, we would say that only a few, such as Moody, were truly great. So why do we call these evangelists great, and how can we be like them?

I've examined that question and found that the answer has little to do with method or technique. Some evangelists preached before the masses, some in churches. Some presented the gospel in small groups, some one on one. Most of the great evangelists used a combination of approaches. But that isn't what made them great.

What I've found is that the great evangelists of the past all shared 10 characteristics that gave them a tremendous heart for the world. Both Scripture and Church history speak to the importance of these characteristics that should shape every Christian's heart and life.

PASSION

First of all, Booth, Calvin, Finney, Luther, Moody, Spurgeon, Sunday, Sung, ten Boom, Wesley, Whitefield, Zinzendorf, Zwingli and all the other truly great evangelists of the past had a passion for souls that burned within them.

Does that same fire burn within you?

"I remind you," Paul says in 2 Timothy 1:6, "to fan into flame the gift of God, which is in you through the laying on of my hands." Why? "For God did not give us a spirit of timidity, but a spirit of power, of love and of self-discipline" (v. 7). The first characteristic that ought to mark us is the fire of the Holy Spirit.

I happened to meet Corrie ten Boom before she went to be with the Lord. I remember she couldn't get up, so I knelt down beside her couch and listened to Corrie say—with that Dutch accent of hers—"I love my Jesus." That phrase still sends shivers down my spine. "I love my Jesus." That love compelled her to proclaim Jesus Christ in more than 60 nations and to lead many thousands to faith in Jesus Christ. What fire for Jesus that woman had! What a passion for souls!

It's possible for us to look at someone we consider great and then simply copy his or her mannerisms and phraseology. The temptation to work up imitation fire instead of experiencing the Holy Spirit's work in our heart can be enormous. This is especially true for those of us trying to reach the masses. We have a desire to be seen. We want to draw attention. But there is a great difference between drawing attention to our Savior and simply calling attention to ourselves.

The men and women whom we call great obviously caught the imagination and attention of the multitudes, but we remember them most because of the impact they made in people's lives. Why? Because the fire of the Holy Spirit burned within them.

GOSPEL

When you read the sermons of the great evangelists of the past, you discover that the evangelists were incredibly Christ-centered. If you look at their messages word for word, it is wonderful how they preached the gospel. I would have given anything to see them in action, proclaiming our Lord Jesus Christ.

You and I are called by God to promote Jesus Christ in this generation. We are His public-relations people. We are His proclaimers,
His ambassadors. We come to town to talk about Jesus, not to be
taken up by sideshows or to enthrall others with our gifts.

How can someone be an evangelist if his or her theme is not
Jesus Christ? Something that evangelist does may be wonderful. It
may be good or intriguing. It may even be of God. *But an evangelist
preaches Jesus Christ.* Some people think that helping the poor is the
gospel, but that's a result of the gospel. Others emphasize healing
the sick. That may be a tremendous sign of God's power, but it isn't
the pure gospel.

Whatever gifts the Spirit gives to you, practice it. But when you
are serving as an evangelist, you must preach Jesus Christ, or you're
not preaching the gospel. You may have an exciting program with
great music, hand clapping, arm waving and people coming forward.
But are you preaching the gospel?

What is the good news that we preach? Paul summarizes it this way:

> I want to remind you of the gospel I preached to you, which
> you received and on which you have taken your stand. By this
> gospel you are saved, if you hold firmly to the word I preached
> to you. Otherwise, you have believed in vain. For what I
> received I passed on to you as of first importance: that Christ
> died for our sins according to the Scriptures, that he was
> buried, that he was raised on the third day according to the
> Scriptures, and that he appeared to Peter, and then to the
> Twelve. After that, he appeared to more than five hundred of
> the brothers at the same time (1 Cor. 15:1-6).

The message of the gospel is that Jesus Christ died for our sins,
was buried and was raised on the third day. Amen? I hope you agree
from the heart. Otherwise, what is your message to the world?

HOLINESS

The great evangelists were holy men and women of God. Now, what is holiness? It isn't a movement. It's a life walked in the light, being transparent before God and others.

Of all the servants of God in the world, evangelists are the most scrutinized. And that's fair enough. If you've tried to hide any sin, confess it and clear it up immediately. After all, the greatest joy is to walk in the light. "If you think sin is fun," Rev. John MacArthur says, "you should try holiness." It's much more exciting.

Don't confuse holiness with the gifts of the Spirit. Some people say, "I must be filled with the Spirit, because I have this or that gift." You can argue with the Lord and say, "But Lord, 35 people came forward last night. Did you hear about the drunkard who was converted?" You can sell yourself on the idea that you must be filled with the Spirit, because so many are coming to faith in Jesus Christ. What a mistake! They're coming to Christ because you preached the gospel, and God always honors the gospel. But what about the state of your own soul?

Billy Graham once pointed out that most evangelists don't last more than 10 years. The temptation to give up is sometimes overwhelming. But more frequently, evangelists don't last because they dishonor the name of the Lord due to a lack of holiness in the areas of money, sex and pride.

I've personally known several powerful evangelists who today are on the sidelines. They're finished. Why? Because they did not walk in holiness. They confused the gift with the walk. There is a big difference.

VISION

Wesley, Moody, Booth and others were men and women with vision. We need to have a big vision, too. It doesn't mean that the Lord will necessarily make you a national or international evangelist, as the journalists might call you, but a large vision gives you perspective and stability. It's like going through a storm in a single-engine airplane. If you've ever flown in such planes, you know they get tossed up and down and side to side by every bit of turbulence. It's terrible, but the pilots love it. Not me. I want smooth sailing.

Now, flying in a jumbo jet is a different story. You look out the window and say, "I love those big wings." They don't get tossed around much in a storm. Those big wings remind me of what it means to have vision. When you have a big vision, the wings move a little, but the airplane doesn't rock very much. If your vision is small, however, your little airplane may feel like it's falling apart. Vision helps you to go through the clouds and the storms without being shaken up and tempted to give up.

Christ certainly never limited His disciples' vision. Even though He restricted His own public ministry to Palestine, He came and died for all mankind. And after His resurrection, He commissioned His followers to "make disciples of all nations" (Matt. 28:19) and sent them to Jerusalem, then to all Judea and Samaria, and ultimately to the ends of the earth.

During the crucial, formative years of the New Testament Church, God used the apostle Paul in a tremendous way. Even his opponents admitted that he had saturated entire provinces with the gospel and turned the world upside down. Why? Because he had a big strategy—big enough to reach the entire Roman Empire, and big enough to give him stability when the going was rough.

During the 1700s, it was Wesley who said, "The world is my parish." He was facing intense opposition across Britain. But, when told to stay in Oxford, Wesley refused to comply. Why should we hide our message and limit our vision when so many have yet to hear the good news of Jesus Christ?

BOLDNESS

Those we call great were men and women with holy audacity. Look at Calvin, who confronted the entire French Church. Luther boldly confronted the Holy Roman Empire. Zinzendorf had the holy audacity to send missionaries and evangelists to the West Indies, and he went, too. Whitefield preached the gospel up and down the British countryside and in America, despite the threat of ridicule and mob violence. These evangelists had holy audacity. Like them, we must learn to launch out in the name of the Lord, take risks, and even face death with courage.

An evangelist is often looked on as a leader within the Body of Christ. Therefore, even under threat, we have to keep going. "I consider my life worth nothing to me," Paul said, "if only I may finish the race and complete the task the Lord Jesus has given me—the task of testifying to the gospel of God's grace" (Acts 20:24).

I've been confronted by militant guerrillas in Peru who threatened to assassinate me. I wanted to get on an airplane and say, "Goodbye, Peru, I'll see you in heaven. Somebody else can evangelize you." In such situations, we have to stop and think, *I'm a servant of the Lord. The Master was crucified. People are looking. I must get on with it in the name of Jesus Christ.*

Holy audacity also prompts us to try new approaches. Some of you may be prepared to use an approach that older folks will question. But you should try it anyway in the name of the Lord. Try it with humility. Try it with counsel. You don't have to do everything the way it has always been done. As far as I'm concerned, any method is valid as long as it is ethical and moral. There are no biblical restraints on methodology (as long as it is done in love), only on the message. The message is sacred, and it never changes. Yet the methods should vary depending on whom we're trying to reach with the gospel.

When you read biographies of the great evangelists, you'll see that they took hold of any method to the end of saturating the cities and the great masses with the gospel. In God's name, they even sanctified the media to communicate the gospel of Jesus Christ.

Somebody asked me the other day, "Do you think if Jesus were here He would be on television?" Of course! If Paul were here, would he have a press conference? Definitely. He would do anything to get the attention of the city.

Those we call great were highly recognized because they took advantage of unique new methods, sanctified them, and used them to evangelize the masses. I believe God wants us to dream about how to use various media to get the attention of people and point them to Jesus Christ.

CRITICISM

From least to greatest, all true evangelists have been criticized, attacked and even persecuted. That shouldn't surprise us, for "everyone who wants to live a godly life in Christ Jesus will be persecuted" (2 Tim. 3:12).

Some people think that as long as you're walking with God, everybody will applaud you and think highly of you. Well, it doesn't work that way. Most people who evangelize create waves. And when you create waves, a lot of people get upset.

What does Scripture say? "Woe to you when all men speak well of you" (Luke 6:26). That's a good verse to remember. It's nice to be well spoken of. I definitely prefer that to criticism. Nevertheless, it's a sign that you're doing something right when certain people begin to get upset because of what you represent and preach.

Calvin saw himself as "only a humble evangelist of our Lord Jesus Christ." But he knew what it was to face severe criticism and attacks. Luther faced intense persecution, too. It wasn't pleasant. But if you read the words of his hymn "A Mighty Fortress Is Our God," you don't pick up a sense of defeat. Instead, Luther seems to be declaring, "I'm going to beat the devil," even though he was running from those who were trying to kill him. And we honor him today.

Spurgeon founded a large church in London, but he was really more of an evangelist than a pastor. He, too, was ridiculed, put down and insulted. Most evangelists are. But when they die, everybody wants to write an article or book saying what great men of God they were.

Even Billy Graham has faced times when people have insulted and cut him down. Yet he's been a godly man. What a marvel to have a man like that who exemplifies integrity and righteousness. He has redeemed the term "evangelist," for during the first half of the twentieth century, to be called an evangelist was an insult in many countries.

CHURCH

When you analyze the great evangelists of the past, you'll find that they saw themselves as active members of the Body of Christ and servants of the Church.

Do you remember what Ephesians 4:11-12 says? God "gave some to be apostles, some to be prophets, some to be evangelists, and some to be pastors and teachers." Why? "To prepare God's people for works of service, so that the body of Christ may be built up."

Our job is to lift up Jesus Christ and build up His Church. We point to sin, but only to show that the Cross liberates us and that the resurrection revolutionizes us. We are not to begin pointing out the flaws and weaknesses of the Church in front of the world.

Unfortunately, a few evangelists actually erred on this point during part of the course of their ministry. Whitefield, for instance, made the mistake of attacking the clergy. We all run that risk if we confuse our calling. Evangelists are not prophets. If you feel called to be a prophet to the Church, don't pretend that you're an evangelist. Learn to differentiate between the two.

An evangelist who really has a burden for the Church will come to revive it by the power of the Holy Spirit. If he has any criticism to make, he makes it privately, behind closed doors, to the leadership.

If I were a pastor, I wouldn't invite an evangelist to my city unless I first found out what church he and his family belonged to and then talked with that church's elders or deacons to find out how active he is within that fellowship. Does he attend when he is home just as everyone else, or does he feel superior because he travels so much? Is he subject to church discipline, or is he exempt because he is better known than the other brothers?

You and I should see ourselves as nothing but slaves of Jesus Christ and servants of His Church. Our goal should be to work with the Church, through the Church and for the Church as we seek to obey Christ's Great Commission.

LOVE

God's greatest servants in the past learned to love the Body of Jesus Christ after they saw their own weaknesses. As the years went by, they realized how much they were growing and learning. Secondary denominational issues weren't as important as they once thought. They began to understand that the Body of Christ includes everyone who belongs to Jesus Christ.

These great servants didn't compromise the basic truth of the gospel. But if you're like me, you may have attended a rather closed fellowship when you were younger in which the feeling was, *We're the only good Christians in town. We know the truth. Everyone else is off track. Why even bother to pray for them?*

As you grow in the Lord, you begin to realize that people who love Jesus Christ are beautiful people. We may not see eye to eye with others on everything, but if we truly know and love Christ, we're all part of the same Body.

What I'm talking about is quite different from phony ecumenism, which hides the truth: "You don't believe Jesus was born of the Virgin Mary? Oh, that's all right. We're one big happy family." There's a difference between that sort of ecumenism and the true unity of the Body of Christ of those who accept the basic truths of Christianity.

What are the basic truths? Read the Apostles' Creed. Anyone who believes those things from a pure heart is a brother or sister in

Christ. Of course, there is much more to believe, too. Some of us get worked up about one point of doctrine, and some about another. But those we call the great evangelists of the past learned that we could afford to have differences on secondary issues.

Secondary issues *are* important. We don't pretend they don't matter to us anymore. For instance, it's plain where I stand on certain issues by the way I speak, by the way I write, by the verses I quote. I don't have to pretend that everyone agrees with me or that I agree with everyone else. We have our convictions. We have our distinctions. We don't give them up, but we say to each other, "I love you in Jesus Christ. I can see the presence of God in your life."

PRAYER

When you read about the great evangelists of the past, you discover that each one learned the secret of prayer in his or her own way. Luther used to get up at four o'clock each morning to pray. Does that mean that you and I need to get up that early, too? Maybe, maybe not. Martin Luther believed, "Just as the business of the tailor is to make clothing, and that of the shoemaker to mend shoes, so the business of the Christian is to pray." The secret of Luther's revolutionary life was his commitment to spend time alone with God every day.

Finney had a prayer partner named Father Nash who traveled with him. Father Nash didn't preach. Most people never knew he was in the town. He often would stay out in the woods praying for Finney morning, noon and night. He prayed for each meeting and for the outpouring of the Holy Spirit of God. What a beautiful thing to have a team member who is faithful and earnest in prayer!

Moody preceded each of his evangelistic campaigns by urging all of God's people to pray. He once said, "We ought to see the face of God every morning before we see the face of man. If you have so much business to attend to that you have no time to pray, depend upon it that you have more business on hand than God ever intended."

FAITHFULNESS

The nine characteristics I've already enumerated actually apply to almost any servant of Jesus Christ. But there is one more characteristic that I want to mention that sets the great evangelists of the past apart from the rest: They evangelized aggressively till their dying hour.

Moody left the pulpit one night absolutely worn out, was sent home immediately under medical care, and died some days later. Whitefield told a friend, "I had rather wear out than rust out." On another occasion he remarked, "I intend going on till I drop." Like Moody, Whitefield died in the middle of an evangelistic campaign.

Billy Graham is another example of faithfulness to the gospel in our own day. About 25 years after Dr. Graham held a crusade in Glasgow, Scotland, we were invited to that city for an evangelistic campaign. There, the story was told of an old Church of Scotland minister who went to hear Dr. Graham each evening. When the crusade was over, the minister said, "Dr. Graham, I've heard you every night for six weeks, and you've preached the same sermon every single night." Except for the introduction and illustrations, that's been true throughout Dr. Graham's worldwide gospel ministry.

An evangelist preaches the same message over and over. There's no variation. Now, our introductory themes may change each time, but eventually about halfway through each message, we speak about the Cross, the resurrection, repentance, faith and commitment. Otherwise, we haven't preached the gospel.

Our sermon titles and introductions and illustrations add color. Other than that, every message is the same. Some Christians may come and say, "Oh, phooey. I've heard this all before." Of course, they have heard it all before! But we're not preaching for them. We're trying to reach the lost.

Scripture tells us that when Jesus saw the lost multitudes, "He had compassion on them, because they were harassed and helpless, like sheep without a shepherd" (Matt. 9:36). We need to ask God to move our hearts with the same compassion that moves His heart.

I believe God desires to cultivate within us a heart that loves the world as He does—enough to keep relentlessly caring whether others hear the gospel, believe in Jesus Christ, and become His disciples.

I trust that you take the Great Commission seriously. When you look at the world around you, what do you see? What has God been saying to your heart? Do you feel His compassion for those without hope and without God in the world?

The Lord is calling us to faithfully fulfill His Great Commission all of our days. Let's press on to finish the task set before us.

CHAPTER 2

CHARACTER COUNTS

SPIRITUAL REQUIREMENTS OF THE EVANGELIST

TIMOTHY ROBNETT

As a college student at Stanford University, I quickly involved myself in a campus ministry. During my junior year, I met Jim Stump, a campus worker and firm believer in focused evangelistic ministry. I still remember the way Jim began when he taught Christians how to use the Four Spiritual Laws to present the gospel: "Have you personally received Jesus Christ's offer of eternal life?"

Jim Stump knew that an effective evangelist has to have dynamic devotion to Jesus Christ. It comes as no surprise that we cannot give away that which we do not possess. If we do not possess a powerful, personal relationship with Jesus Christ, how can we transfer the joy of that relationship to another person?

Think of it this way: A friend is planning her summer vacation and asks for your help. When she inquires about Hawaii, you describe the beauty that covers every inch of the islands, but you can't offer much more than that because you've never been there. Like your friend, you can only imagine the real-life experience.

But if you *have* been to Hawaii, you can then describe the brilliant sun, bright colors and bold flavors with confidence and authority. You are genuine when you say, "I have tasted and I have seen." Likewise, an evangelist who practices a genuine relationship with Christ has "tasted and seen that the LORD is good" (Ps. 34:8). Until we practice dynamic devotion to God, we cannot effectively share His truth with those who do not know Him. Like the advice we give to our vacationing friend, we can only offer a searching soul the travel-brochure description of salvation.

Like any relationship, dynamic devotion to God requires discipline. Healthy spiritual growth is never stagnant. Like a blooming plant or a growing child, our relationship with God requires constant nourishment and care. So, to be effective evangelists, how should we grow in our relationship with Christ?

Through His Word

As director of Next Generation Alliance® (NGA), I coordinate and attend a variety of ministry meetings throughout the year. While hosting one particular NGA conference in Fort Lauderdale, I was both discouraged and delighted by a conversation I had with the hotel supervisor.

As we worked out the set-up details of our next general meeting, the supervisor thanked me for bringing such a courteous and helpful group to the hotel. "This is the way we act," I explained to him, "because we represent Jesus Christ in all that we do."

"We have a lot of Christian groups hold meetings here," replied the supervisor, "but not all of them are like your group."

Now, I cannot guess at the specific conduct of those other Christian groups, but it was obvious that they did not leave a favorable impression on the hotel staff. This discouraged me, because I believe that Christian conduct is informed by God's Word and empowered by God's Spirit.

Just as those attending the conference represent Jesus Christ to the hotel staff, the evangelist constantly represents the gospel to the world. How can we represent Christ if we do not root our conduct in deeper knowledge of His character? How can we reflect the Spirit of Christ without a growing intimacy with Him, which comes from knowledge of His words? The Word of God is not a tool in a toolbox, helpful for certain tasks but useless for others. The Bible dynamically and continually transforms us into the witnesses that God wants us to be. Evangelists must be students of the Scriptures if we are to maximize our effectiveness for the good news.

Biblical knowledge also enables us to fully explain and defend the gospel. Just days before Operation Iraqi Freedom, television broadcaster Larry King asked five Christian leaders to discuss God's position on war. I identified most with Max Lucado, who gave a clear statement of his position, complete with biblical evidence and clear logic. He spoke compassionately, with complete respect for those with differing opinions.

The apostle Peter encourages this kind of biblical defense: While we must always be ready to give an account of our faith, we must do so "with gentleness and respect" (1 Pet. 3:15).

May 2000 found the Palau team in Shanghai, China, with many sensitive issues surrounding the team's first public visit to the nation. In a message to the Moen Church, Luis preached from Acts 9, using Paul's conversion to highlight God's desire to reach even those who resist Jesus Christ and persecute His people. What a message to preach in Shanghai before many who intimately knew the pain of persecution and many government officials who committed those acts. But Luis preached with confidence, knowing that his words were grounded in Scripture, which can pierce the hardest heart. Although Luis could not make a public invitation, the success of that meeting is evident, as national Christian leaders invited the Palau team back to minister in Beijing in April 2004.

Paul exhorts Timothy, "Preach the Word; be prepared in season and out of season" (2 Tim. 4:2). When we are intimately connected in every season of life to Christ and His Word, we can demonstrate the gospel with our lives, defend the faith that we preach, speak boldly of the times in which we live, and give powerful evangelistic messages preached directly from Scripture.

THROUGH OUR PRAYERS

After serving as an NGA partner evangelist for several years, Mike Silva was ready to return the favor. In 2000, Mike Silva and his team experienced great success in preaching the gospel in Trichy, India; shortly afterward, Mike was invited back to India to preach in Madurai. Now that God had opened the doors, Mike was ready to throw them wide open. With the help of NGA, Mike placed evangelists in several surrounding cities, creating a regional evangelistic effort that culminated in Madurai's huge Good News Festival. All together, NGA partnering evangelists preached to 102,000 people in 10 days, with some 17,000 individuals committing their lives to Jesus Christ.

Several of those evangelists planned a return trip to India in February 2003. However, this time nothing was the same. Government officials enforced a strict "no conversion" law and forbade all public religious activity. Still, the desire remained: God was calling these evangelists back to southern India.

Unsure of what lay ahead, but sure of their purpose, the evangelists started to pray, and they did not stop praying until they returned home. Where violent threats put pastors and evangelists at risk, God provided greater security. Where evangelists could not preach the message outdoors, God enabled local pastors to deliver that same message within church buildings. Where relations with the Indian government seemed tenuous at best, God provided daily meetings between Christian leaders and government officials to ensure safety for all involved.

Satan wants to destroy the work of evangelism and he will do anything to keep us from answering the Great Commission. Prayer is our mightiest weapon in fighting these evil schemes. Guardians of the gospel pray faithfully, because we know prayer destroys the strongholds that hold back evangelistic ministry. By building a network of prayer warriors to protect our ministries, we activate the power of God.

THROUGH THE CHURCH

Many evangelists feel shunned by the Church. I do not understand all the issues that may explain this feeling, but I can tell you countless stories of evangelists who feel frustration, a lack of acceptance, and a sense of uselessness when working with the Church.

One particular story comes to mind. A dear friend of mine found that after years of theological training, internships and ministry work in North America, he could not find a ministry position suited for his evangelistic gifting. When God finally opened a door for my friend to work in Europe, he eagerly followed that path. Now, some 30 years later, he still preaches Jesus Christ worldwide and has a growing ministry for emerging evangelists in Europe.

I do not doubt God's sovereign hand of guidance in my friend's ministry career. But I have to wonder: If it took my friend several frustrating years—and ultimately, an international move—to find suitable evangelistic work, how many times has the Church lost a gifted individual like him to the frustration of not finding a job?

Regardless of past injustice or present frustration, evangelists must love the Church. I'm not talking only about the place of worship that they attend each week. Evangelists must have a deep love for the whole Church—the entire body of believers. And I'm not talking only about emotional love for the Church. To love the body of believers is an act of service—to live and act in such a way that the life of the Church matures. Consider these verses from Ephesians: "It was he who gave some to be . . . evangelists . . . to prepare God's people for works of service, so that the body of Christ may be built up" (Eph. 4:11-12). If we love the Church, our goal will always be to build up the Church, not tear it down.

How do we build up the body of believers? First, we must honor the Church and her leadership with encouragement and support. Brad Butcher, an NGA emerging evangelist, is one of the best examples of this relationship. Brad is often asked to speak at evangelistic youth events. In this type of situation, it is easy (and quite common) for speakers to show up at the event, give a message, and then leave. But when Brad accepts a speaking engagement, he commits to:

· Work together with the youth staff to prepare the event. This includes mobilizing a prayer team, formatting a schedule of events, and even coordinating room logistics when necessary.

- Serve the church by doing his homework. When Brad delivers a message, he does not pull out a cookie-cutter gospel presentation. Instead, he puts in time beforehand to tailor the message to his audience while still clearly focusing on the person of Jesus Christ.

- Implement a follow-up strategy for new believers. Working together with the church, Brad develops a timetable and materials to support new believers in getting involved with the church and growing in a new relationship with Christ.

Another powerful way to encourage the Church is to strengthen the community of church leaders. A positive way to do this is to use the gift of recognition: During an event, ask all church leaders in the group to stand, and then take a moment to thank these individuals for their service to the Body of Christ and pray for them.

Conducting a seminar for pastors and leaders is a more time-intensive but equally fruitful ministry of encouragement. In almost every city he visits, Mike Silva incorporates a training seminar into his festival schedule. These seminars are designed not to evangelize but to equip and encourage, and they often lead to long-term relationships between local churches and between those churches and Mike Silva. Mike has realized the power of the Church's support to make his an effective evangelistic ministry.

We must also build the Church by seeking her partnership in our ministry. By accepting invitations given by local church leaders, we embark on a partnership with those leaders to reach their community for Jesus Christ. It has been my experience that when we work together with local pastors, we maximize the effectiveness of any evangelistic event.

Once the Luis Palau Association accepts an invitation to conduct an evangelistic festival, we utilize the people power in a community to make the event happen. When Luis Palau shared the good news in

Kingston, Jamaica, a team of 143 local church members traveled with us from the United States to work as event volunteers, prayer warriors and counselors at the various festivals. The Jamaica festivals were a success not only because of the Luis Palau Association or our volunteers but also because of the hard work of every church member throughout Jamaica who participated in leading the event.

I'll never forget one of my first experiences as a member of the Luis Palau team. It was October 1990, and we were in Des Moines, Iowa. While standing in the lobby of the civic center after one of Luis's evening meetings, a local believer walked up to me and shared these thoughts: "I have waited so many years to be trained in personal evangelism and participate in such a great event as this. Thank you so much for helping me become more effective as a witness for Christ." Local church members benefit greatly when the evangelist and his team prepare them for effectively sharing Christ.

A third mechanism for building the Church is to build a bridge between decision makers and the local church community. Our job as evangelists goes only so far, but the spiritual life of every individual who accepts Christ at one of our events has just begun. By directing these new believers into local churches, we establish not only a relationship between the new believer and a local body of believers but also build up our relationship with each church and her leadership.

Jesus stated His purpose with these words: "I will build my church" (Matt. 16:18). As an evangelist, what will be your relationship with the Church? Will you honor and serve her? Will you build up the body of believers?

Through Our Fellowship

Another powerful component of any evangelist's ministry is his or her commitment to fellowship. In addition to faithful participation in the life of his home church in Portland, Oregon, for the past three decades Luis Palau has built relationships through a men's prayer group. Although he travels half of the year, Luis meets with his group when he is home and prays with them no matter the distance.

On more than one occasion, this prayer group has come to the rescue. When Luis's wife, Pat, was diagnosed with cancer, his prayer group rallied around the family and prayed fervently for Pat's treatment. When his son Andrew entered college and began living on the wild side, prayer powerfully influenced Andrew's dramatic return to Christ. One small fellowship of faithful men has been a mighty influence on Luis's courage to serve God as an evangelist.

Like Luis, many evangelists travel frequently and struggle to cultivate long-term relationships. Effective evangelists must seek out godly men and women for fellowship and partnership in ministry. We need a support system, even if it contradicts our sense of self-sufficiency. These relationships must foster mutual respect, affirmation and exhortation. Our support system may be a prayer group, Bible study, or an accountability group. Whatever it is, get involved in the life of your church and participate in the fellowship of believers. If an evangelist of Luis Palau's stature admits his need for the support of other believers, then I assure you, we all need fellowship.

Effective evangelists also find great wisdom and encouragement by seeking out older, experienced evangelists as mentors. Next Generation Alliance exists to connect evangelists in these relationships. When Mike Silva first began serving the Lord as an NGA partner evangelist, Dr. Bill Thomas came alongside to support and mentor Mike's growing ministry. Dr. Thomas's extensive knowledge and experience in international evangelism allowed Mike to learn about preaching the gospel in underdeveloped countries, and over time, those countries became the focus of Mike's ministry. Now that Mike himself mentors newly emerging evangelists, Dr. Thomas has taken three more young servants under his wing to teach them about international evangelistic ministry.

In just a few years, NGA has seen a number of its partner evangelists grow in ministry through mentoring relationships with Luis

Palau and other Palau team members. Such healthy mentoring relationships may last for a season or a lifetime, but either way, they must build mutual respect and encouragement, foster spiritual growth, and help people develop professional skills. (You may already have someone in mind for this mentoring role; if not, please use the information at the back of this book to contact NGA and get connected with an experienced evangelist.)

Effective evangelists commit to ongoing spiritual growth and maturity by reading the Bible, engaging in prayer, loving the Church, and participating in fellowship. If we do not commit to these activities, we put our ministry at risk. I have seen too many evangelists find security in their performance for Jesus Christ, not their position in Christ. Paul warns against performance-driven ministry in 2 Corinthians 3:1-5: "Are we beginning to commend ourselves again? Do we need . . . letters of recommendation?" No, he tells the people of Corinth. True evangelistic success is not measured by our own skill, "but our competence comes from God."

When performance drives ministry, the acceptance of others becomes our Achilles' heel. Evangelists become people-pleasers, not God-pleasers. Charisma and success supplant relationship and intimacy with God. But when position in Christ drives ministry, we develop our sense of security as gifted evangelists. We seek only to please God, not men. Our dynamic devotion to God becomes visible in all that we say and do.

When we focus our relationship with Jesus Christ on His Word, prayer, the Church and fellowship with other evangelists, we build the foundation of an effective and lasting evangelistic ministry.

CHAPTER 3

VISION FOR THE WORLD

THE MISSION OF THE EVANGELIST

LUIS PALAU

Have you ever tasted a nice, cool, refreshing Coke®? Congratulations! So have hundreds of millions of other people all around the world. And it's all Robert Woodruff's fault.

Well, not all his fault. But he's largely to blame.

You see, Woodruff served as president of Coca-Cola from 1923 to 1955. During World War II, while serving as chief executive of that soft-drink corporation, he had the audacity to state, "We will see that every man in uniform gets a bottle of Coca-Cola for five cents wherever he is and whatever it costs." After World War II ended, Woodruff went on to say that in his lifetime, he wanted *everyone* in the world to have a taste of Coca-Cola. Talk about vision!

With careful planning and a lot of persistence, Woodruff and his colleagues reached their generation around the globe for Coke.

How big is your vision? Have you ever thought about what God could do through you to influence our own generation?

I'm not kidding. Neither was the Lord Jesus Christ kidding when He called His disciples to gain a vision of impacting the world for His name.

The Twelve (minus Judas) listened intently as Christ sought to prepare them for His imminent betrayal and subsequent death. "No matter what happens," He told them, "believe in Me. I am the Way and the Truth and the Life. I am in the Father and He is in Me. We work in unity. If you can't believe My words alone, at least believe Me because of the miracles you have seen" (see John 14: 1-11). Then the Lord startled the apostles with the words of John 14:12-15:

> I tell you the truth, anyone who has faith in me will do what I have been doing. He will do even greater things than these, because I am going to the Father. And I will do whatever you ask in my name, so that the Son may bring glory to the Father. You may ask me for anything in my name, and I will do it. If you love me, you will obey what I command.

Don't underestimate those words. Read them again. Here in capsule form Christ challenges His disciples—and that now includes you and me—to dream great dreams, plan great plans, pray great prayers and obey His great commands.

DREAM GREAT DREAMS

In the disciples' minds, time was fast running out. For more than three years, they had hoped Christ would be the one who would redeem Israel and reign as Messiah. But now, Jesus was saying that one of them would betray Him and deliver Him up to the Jewish leaders to be crucified.

They couldn't accept what He was telling them: "I will be with you only a little longer." "I am going to My Father." "I am leaving you." Everything within them screamed, *No! This can't be true!*

So imagine what the Twelve thought when Christ went on to promise, "I tell you the truth, anyone who has faith in me will do what I have been doing" (v. 12).

Around the Upper Room table sat Peter, who had almost drowned trying to walk on water. And Philip, who waved his arms in exclamation when stating the impossibility of buying enough bread to feed the multitude. And Andrew, who, with a number of the other disciples, had not been able to heal a boy who was demon possessed.

To each disciple, Christ said, "You can continue the work I have been doing." And His promise is the same to you and me. He calls us to dream great dreams of what we can do to impact our world for His glory. How is this possible? The key is twofold.

First, because Christ was going to the Father, He assured the disciples that He would send the Comforter, the Holy Spirit, to indwell all believers. Christ would now continue His work through us!

Second, Christ qualified His promise with a condition. Notice that He said, "Anyone *who has faith in me* will do what I have been doing." The Lord challenges us to have faith—not necessarily more faith, but to have faith in Him. It is an ongoing faith. The *Williams New Testament* puts it this way: "Whoever perseveres in believing in me can himself do the things that I am doing."[1]

Have you stopped seeing great things happen in your life? Perhaps you have stopped believing that God can work in a mighty way in our generation. But what limits the work of God here on Earth? Is God somehow incapable of renewing the churches in America? Of turning the hearts of thousands upon thousands to Himself? Of causing the fires of revival to spread throughout this country and beyond? Of course not! Yet, God has chosen to limit His works—at least in some measure—to those things we trust Him to do through us.

Why is it that so few Christians ever accomplish great things for Christ? I believe it is because Christians too often lose the ability to dream great dreams. I see it happening all the time.

New believers are notorious for their enthusiasm and almost childlike trust in God. Accounts of heroes of the faith such as George Müller, Hudson Taylor, Corrie ten Boom and Dawson Trotman inspire them to step out and attempt what others consider presumptuous. But as time goes by, hardening of the spiritual arteries sets in, and they become cynical. They lose the joy and thrill of the Christian life. They hear of something wonderful happening and say, "Oh?" as if it were really nothing.

How nonchalant we become about God's work around the world! Oh, our doctrinal statements still sound theologically correct, but our lives deny the reality we profess.

In order for God to use us again, we need to confess our unbelief and say, "Lord Jesus, renew my vision of Your power. Renew my confidence in Your abilities. Renew my trust in Your resources." Then begin to dream again!

As previously mentioned, Christ Himself never limited His disciples' vision. But the Early Church did what we all do—they hesitated to dream about what God wanted to do in their own generation.

It finally took the stoning of Stephen and subsequent conversion of Saul to shake them out of their complacency.

While other believers scattered throughout Palestine, the apostle Paul took Christ's Great Commission seriously and devoted the latter half of his life to traveling and proclaiming the gospel to the Gentiles.

In Romans 15, Paul records a summary of his first missionary journey. He had already given detailed oral reports to the church in Antioch (see Acts 14:27) and to the Jerusalem Council (see Acts 15:12). But in Romans 15, he simply states, "From Jerusalem all the way around to Illyricum, I have fully proclaimed the gospel of Christ" (v. 19).

Now, the distance from Jerusalem to Illyricum is some 750 miles over land. Yet Paul could look back on that trip and say, "Mission accomplished. I have fully proclaimed the gospel in that entire area." Paul didn't stop, however, and assume there wasn't anything left to do. Instead, he was already dreaming of the mission fields beyond.

Where have your own dreams stopped? Have they been lost somewhere between your living room and the house next door? If your dreams aren't greater than finishing your education, paying your bills, or raising your children, then your vision isn't divine. Maybe it's time to consider how God could use you to make a difference in the lives of others.

Opportunities to serve Christ abound if we take God at His word and plan to accomplish great things by His power working through us.

PLAN GREAT PLANS

When I was about 17 years old and beginning to take the Word of God seriously, John 14:12 really bothered me. I just couldn't believe what the second half of the verse says. I even checked other translations to see if I could find a better rendering. But the verse reads essentially the same in every version of the Bible.

Jesus Christ declares, "He [who believes in me] will do even greater things than these [which I have done], because I am going to the Father" (John 14:12). That is a fantastic, almost incredible, yet true promise. It came from the lips of the Lord Jesus and has been proved trustworthy many times. Christ promises that we can do *greater* works than He did!

Perhaps another look at the ministry of Paul will help us better understand what Christ is saying here. Without a doubt, God used Paul tremendously during the crucial, formative years of the New Testament Church. Even his opponents admitted that Paul had saturated entire provinces with the gospel (see Acts 19:26) and turned the world upside down (see Acts 17:6).

Some scholars have even claimed that, from a human point of view, this Pharisee-turned-preacher influenced history more than Jesus Christ Himself. In his book *From Guilt to Glory*, Ray Stedman writes, "Did you ever stop to ask yourself what influence the Apostle Paul has had in your own life? He lived nearly two thousand years ago, and yet there is not one person among us who has not had his life drastically affected by this man. The whole course of history has been changed by the truths he taught." [2]

How would you like your church to support a missionary like *that*?

What was Paul's secret? Simple. He wasn't just a dreamer. He also planned great plans and carried them out in the power of the Holy Spirit. Those plans included utilizing ministry teams, traveling extensively, taking advantage of opportunities to witness for Christ, and establishing local churches to nurture new believers.

You see, Paul wasn't content to saturate one small area with the gospel at the expense of the rest of the world. He had a strategy for reaching the entire Roman Empire! He could say, "But now that there is no more place for me to work in these regions [Jerusalem to Illyricum], and since I have been longing for many years to see you [in Rome], I plan to do so when I go to Spain" (Rom. 15:23-24).

Paul goes on in that chapter to explain his itinerary. In his mind he could visualize every major city that he would stop at on his way to Rome. He longed to eventually win the people of that capital city to Christ. But beyond that, his ultimate goal was to reach Spain—the western limit of the empire.

Notice that the apostle used strategic thinking to fulfill his ministry. He didn't consider it carnal or beneath his dignity to plan strategically. Instead, he used it as a tool to reach the masses more effectively.

I can remember how frustrated I felt as a young man, thinking about evangelizing the unsaved. *Lord, there are millions of people who don't know You. Yet here we sit, Sunday after Sunday, the same people doing the same things. We have to do something.* So several of us began to pray together. "Lord, move us to reach out to the lost. Use us by Your Spirit." Slowly, in my heart and in the hearts of others, a vision began to grow—a vision of winning thousands of people to Christ.

Some of my own dreams were so wild that I didn't tell anyone but my mother about them—and I didn't tell her all of them. She encouraged us, saying, "Come on, you don't need a special message from the Lord before moving out to reach the lost. He gave the order centuries ago to preach the good news to everyone. So go. Don't keep waiting for more instructions."

So we began to evangelize slowly, in a small way. Now I'm amazed when I realize how the Lord has already fulfilled so many of our biggest dreams. "Praise the Lord" is all I can say. "It really happened by His power."

Of course, we must continually recognize God's role in our planning. Psalm 127:1 reminds us, "Unless the LORD builds the house, its builders labor in vain"—no matter how nice a job the architect did on the blueprints.

I believe God encourages us to make plans based on wise and godly counsel. As you read Isaiah, for instance, you will notice that while God condemns the schemes of the wicked (see 30:1),

He commends the plans of the upright (see 32:8)—even though He ordained everything long ago (see 37:26).

Our planning is never intended to replace God's sovereign leading in our lives. Paul demonstrated this in his own ministry. Yes, he had a definite strategy for letting all of the Roman Empire hear the voice of God, but he was not bound to his plans. He remained sensitive to the Spirit's leading. For example, remember how the Spirit compelled him to go to Macedonia, even though he had other plans (see Acts 16:6-10)?

This is an exciting concept to me. On the one hand, God intends for us to use logical, strategic planning in fulfilling the Great Commission. But on the other hand, God can redirect our plans when necessary. One doesn't necessarily cancel out the need for the other.

Do you have dreams and plans of what God might do through your life? Or are you just busy with life's routine, ordinary tasks? Have you become bored—or boring?

The Lord Jesus Christ challenges us to abandon our complacency when He says, "You can do even greater things than I have done through My Spirit who indwells you." He doesn't intend for us to sit idly and simply dream of what could happen for His glory. He wants us to plan great plans so that those dreams can come true!

William Carey upset the status quo of the Church in his day when he proposed sending missionaries from Britain to evangelize other parts of the world. Older Christians told him to give up his preposterous ideas. Carey countered their boredom and doubt by writing, "Expect great things from God, attempt great things for God." That statement became the creed of the modern missions movement as men and women followed Carey's example and went to the ends of the earth with the saving message of Christ's gospel. God wants us to attempt great things for Him to reach our generation.

Over the years, God has stretched my own vision. At first, God burdened my heart for the city of Cordoba, where I lived as a young man, then neighboring areas, then all of Argentina. Finally, I dreamed of preaching the gospel throughout all of Latin America.

But God wasn't through with me yet. Today, in faith, our evangelistic association wants to let the whole world hear the voice of God. With that dream in mind, we are planning massive festivals, multiplied by daily radio and television specials, and sports evangelism to reach large segments of the world's population. And by God's grace, as partners in evangelism with other Christians and their churches and organizations, we are seeing thousands of lives changed!

What about you? Are you expecting great things from God? Or are you letting the opportunities pass you by? If it's true that the Lord wants the gospel preached worldwide, we can't remain passive. Whatever our gifts or abilities or resources, we need to work together as faithful stewards of what God has bestowed on us.

Dream a little. Envision the 190 million Americans who have not accepted the gospel in this generation. Many have never even heard it clearly explained. What are you going to do about it?

Start doing something by making specific plans of action. Determine how God could use you to share Christ at work, at school, in your neighborhood—and beyond. Remember, God wants to use you. Let Him!

Pray Great Prayers

Years ago, I read about this amazing invention called "television" in *Time* magazine and dreamed about how it could be used to broadcast the gospel to literally millions of people. Little did I realize how effective this tool would become in our mass evangelistic festivals.

A wealthy friend of mine who loves the Lord is excited about reaching people through television. Some years ago he told me, "Luis, any time you have an evangelistic campaign overseas, I'll pay for one night of broadcasting. If I can, I'll pay for two or three nights."

It's nice to have friends like that! But to be honest with you, I had the hardest time calling him. So every once in a while, he called me. "Hey, don't you have any festivals going? You haven't called me. Don't you need any money?"

Well, of course we had campaigns going, and of course we needed money to broadcast the gospel. But for some reason, I was hesitant to call him.

We're like that with the Lord, too. You see, the Lord doesn't simply tell us to dream great dreams and plan great plans. He adds, "And I will do whatever you ask in my name, so that the Son may bring glory to the Father. You may ask me for anything in my name, and I will do it" (John 14:13-14).

The Lord wants us to ask Him for anything in His name. *Anything!* He says it not once, but twice. "Look," He says, "I'm going to repeat Myself so you will know I mean it. Go ahead and pray great prayers, and watch Me make it happen."

Like other promises throughout Scripture, this one comes with a condition. "And I will do whatever you ask in my name, so that the Son may *bring glory to the Father.*" That's the key: If we ask so that the Father will be glorified, He'll answer. That's why when we pray for the opportunities and the resources needed to call others to Christ we can rest assured that God won't let us down. He takes delight in answering our petitions.

When my youngest son, Stephen, was only six years old, like all other boys that age he had a million requests. He asked me for some of the craziest things. Some of his requests were too much, of course, but I didn't mind. I loved to have him come and ask me anyway. Generally, if I could afford what he wanted, I gave it to him. He's my son.

Our heavenly Father also wants us to come to Him with our requests. And He loves to answer us. Christ said it best when He explained, "If you, then, though you are evil, know how to give good gifts to your children, how much more will your Father in heaven give good gifts to those who ask him!" (Matt. 7:11).

"I will do whatever you ask." I have claimed that promise many times during my life. One of my first requests was for a coin for a bus ride to work in Argentina. God didn't miraculously drop a coin out of heaven, but He did supply a ride in an unusual way.

God has continued to answer many of my prayers—prayers for big decisions, desperate needs, safety, personnel, wisdom. Answers to those prayers, whether big or small, have caused my faith to grow and grow.

While we were planning a festival in Nicaragua several years ago, God demonstrated His willingness to answer our greatest prayers. At first, the budget for the mass evangelistic effort allowed only for limited radio coverage of the meetings. That was enlarged to become a satellite radio network reaching 20 Spanish-speaking countries. Then someone suggested, "Why don't we use television, too? Blanket the entire continent!"

As the magnitude of that vision for reaching 200 million Spanish-speaking people with the gospel at one time—and the realization that it would cost us $200,000—hit us, with one accord we went to our knees before the Lord. In prayer, we committed the immense under-taking to God and asked Him to supply the finances we needed. We rose from our knees confident that He would provide.

And He did! When the bills were in and the accounting complet-ed, the needed $200,000 had come in, almost to the penny!

A year later, we again enlarged our vision for evangelism and asked the Lord for half a million dollars. It seemed like a ridiculous amount for a bunch of missionaries to request. Still, we believed the Lord would provide.

But then I had second thoughts. Oh, I still wanted the Lord to meet our financial needs, but I couldn't bring myself to come right out with John 14:13-14 in front of me and say, "Lord Jesus, You told me to ask for anything, and I'm asking you for $500,000."

Instead, I began to sell the Lord on our vision. I whittled it down, saying, "Lord, if you could send $20,000 this month, because we're having a crusade in Mexico, and then next month if you could send . . ." Suddenly, I realized, *How stupid! The Lord knows all our plans. I'm not going to break any news to Him if I tell Him we need half a million dollars.*

Christ said, "I will do whatever you ask in My name." Whatever we ask! He didn't say, "Sell Me on your idea; convince Me that I should give you what you want." He merely said, "Ask."

I confessed to the Lord my disobedience and asked Him for half a million dollars, and He provided again!

OBEY GREAT COMMANDS

The Lord Jesus Christ has been calling His disciples to gain a vision for evangelism. He's been encouraging them to dream great dreams, plan great plans and pray great prayers. But that's not all.

Christ offers one further word of encouragement: "If you love me, you will obey what I command" (John 14:15).

At first glance, His statement seems out of place. Unlike the preceding three verses in John 14 that we've considered, this one isn't a promise. Or is it?

The context of this passage gives us a clue. In verse 21 we read, "Whoever has my commands and obeys them, he is the one who loves me. He who loves me will be loved by my Father, and I too will love him and show myself to him." In other words, we experience God's love when we obey His commands. That's a promise worth remembering!

The value of doing what we have been told—for our own good—was illustrated vividly for me in early 1983 when more than 90 people conducted an all-night search for an eight-year-old boy named Dominic. While on a skiing trip with his father, this little boy apparently had ridden a new lift and skied off the run without realizing it. The search party hoped to find Dominic somewhere on the snowy mountain slope before it was too late.

As each hour passed, the search party and the boy's family became more and more concerned. By dawn, they still had found no trace of him. Two helicopters joined the search, and within 15 minutes, the rescuers spotted ski tracks. A ground team was sent to follow the tracks, which changed to small footprints. The footprints eventually led to a tree, where at last they found the boy.

"He's in super shape," Sgt. Terry Silbaugh, the area search and rescue coordinator, announced to the anxious family and press. "In fact, he's in better shape than we are right now." A hospital spokesman said the boy was in fine condition. He wasn't even admitted to the hospital.

Silbaugh explained why the boy did so well despite spending a night in the freezing elements. His father had enough foresight to warn the boy what to do if he became lost, and his son had enough trust to do exactly what his father said.

Dominic protected himself from possible frostbite and hypothermia by snuggling up to a tree and covering himself with branches. As a young child, he never would have thought of doing this on his own. He was simply obeying his wise and loving father.[3]

Dominic reminds me of what we should do as children of our loving and wise heavenly Father. We are not to walk according to the course of this world, which is passing away. Instead, we are to walk in obedience to the Lord's commands. After all, He knows what is best for us. That's one of the reasons I believe the Bible is so relevant for us today. It gives us God's commands.

The apostle Peter talks about this near the beginning of his first letter. He tells us, "As obedient children, do not conform to the evil desires you had when you lived in ignorance. But just as he who called you is holy, so be holy in all you do; for it is written: 'Be holy, because I am holy'" (1 Pet. 1:14-16).

You might be thinking, *But isn't Peter—impulsive, denying Peter— being a bit idealistic? How does he really expect us to achieve such obedience and holiness while here on Earth?*

Some Christians feel they can attain Peter's exhortation if they work hard enough and pray long enough. But that's the essence of legalism. As sincere as legalists may be, if they are relying on their own power and not on the indwelling Christ, then they are headed for a terrible fall.

This was the case with Moses when he killed the Egyptian who had been beating a Hebrew slave. Moses was sincere in his intentions, but he was relying on his own power, the weapons of the flesh.

This was my own situation when I came to the United States in 1961 to further my biblical studies at Multnomah School of the Bible. I had big dreams that I wanted to see quickly accomplished. My impatience led me to rely on my own power, not the Lord's.

During one of the last chapel services at school before the end of the term, our speaker was Major Ian Thomas, founder of the Torchbearers in England. Major Thomas's theme was "Any Old Bush Will Do, As Long As God Is in the Bush."

He pointed out that it took Moses 40 years in the wilderness to get to the point that he was nothing. God was trying to tell Moses, "I don't need a pretty bush or an educated bush or an eloquent bush. Any old bush will do, as long as I am in the bush. If I am going to use you, I am going to use you. It will not be you doing something for Me, but Me doing something through you."

Major Thomas suggested that the bush in the desert was likely a dry bunch of ugly little sticks that had hardly developed, yet God told Moses to take off his shoes. Why? Because this was holy ground. Why? Because God was in the bush!

I was like that bush. I could do nothing for God. All my reading, studying, asking questions and trying to model myself after others was worthless. Everything in my ministry was worthless unless God was in me! No wonder I felt so frustrated. Only He could make something happen.

It all came together when Major Thomas closed with Galatians

2:20: "I have been crucified with Christ and I no longer live, but Christ lives in me. The life I live in the body, I live by faith in the Son of God, who loved me and gave himself for me." I realized that the secret to being an obedient, holy Christian was to depend on the indwelling, resurrected, almighty Lord Jesus, and not on myself. God was finally in control of this bush!

I had tremendous peace, because I realized that I didn't have to struggle to be holy. How sad that I had wasted eight years of my life trying to do everything in my own power.

But just because we cannot work to become holy—any more than we can work for our salvation—doesn't mean we should quench the Spirit and do nothing!

When I think about Christians who sit still or stand around when God wants them to act, speak and move, I am reminded of Bill Fuqua. In case you haven't heard about Fuqua, he is the current *Guinness Book of World Records* champion at doing nothing. He appears so absolutely still during his routines at shopping malls, fairgrounds and amusement parks that he's sometimes mistaken for a mannequin.

Fuqua discovered his unique talent at the age of 14 when, as a joke, he stood motionless in front of a Christmas tree. A woman touched him and exclaimed, "Oh! I thought it was a real person."

Do people question whether you're a real Christian? If you are a true disciple of Christ, you will willingly and eagerly obey the Lord Jesus' great commands. After all, the first step in the Christian life is confessing "Jesus as Lord" (Rom. 10:9). Indeed, the day is coming when "every tongue [shall] confess that Jesus Christ is Lord" (Phil. 2:11). Why? Because God the Father has given Jesus supremacy over all creation (see Col. 1:18). Christ is the very "King of kings and Lord of lords" (1 Tim. 6:15).

Every subsequent step in the Christian life involves obeying Jesus as Lord. The apostle John tells us, "We know that we have come to know him if we obey his commands" (1 John 2:3). To the degree that we know and believe Jesus is Lord, we obey Him. The Bible calls this the fear of the Lord.

The fear of the Lord implies a deep reverence and awe of God—and a corresponding response of obedience. Psalm 112:1 says, "Blessed is the man who fears the LORD, who finds great delight in his commands."

Christ knew that the obedience of His disciples depended on their conviction that He was—and is—the Lord. That's why after His resurrection, He began His last words to them with the declaration, "All authority in heaven and on earth has been given to me" (Matt. 28:18). Because He is the Lord of lords, He has every right to issue great commands.

Then Christ adds, "Therefore go and make disciples of all nations, baptizing them in the name of the Father and of the Son and of the Holy Spirit, and teaching them to obey everything I have commanded" (Matt. 28:19-20). We often refer to this as the "Great Commission." But actually, His commands are always great. He never gives little, puny suggestions.

Because of the great commands we have received from Christ, our vision as Christians should be to win as many people as possible to Jesus Christ throughout the world. Investment advisor Austin Pryor tells how God changed his priorities:

> As I began to get more burdened about the great commission, business concerns couldn't compete. Let's say you're a marketing person: You can either spend your life trying to get more people to drink Coke or you can spend your life trying to help fulfill the great commission. There's no comparison. It captures your imagination, your affections, your energies. You want to invest in it. I began to feel that commodities trading wasn't important enough for me to be spending that much time on. Eventually, it fell by the wayside.[4]

Evangelism is not an option in the Christian life. Paul admitted, "Yet when I preach the gospel, I cannot boast, for I am compelled to preach. Woe to me if I do not preach the gospel!" (1 Cor. 9:16).

THE GREATEST THRILL

A day came in my own life when I decided I didn't have the gift of evangelism. It was obvious. I had been zealously preaching the gospel in Argentina, but no one was coming to Christ. Nothing I did seemed to make a difference. I was inspired by the things I read and heard about Billy Graham's ministry, but I knew I didn't have whatever he had.

I gave God a deadline: "If I don't see any converts through my preaching by the end of the year, I'm quitting." Oh, I would still be an obedient Christian, but I would bypass the Great Commission and other verses and resign myself simply to teaching other believers.

The end of the year came and went. No converts. My mind was made up—I was through evangelizing. Now I was sure that I didn't have the gift.

On Saturday morning, about four days into the new year, the small church I attended held a home Bible study. I didn't feel like going, but I went anyway out of loyalty to the elders. The fellow who was supposed to lead the Bible study didn't come. So the man of the house said, "Luis, you are going to have to say something." I was completely unprepared.

I had been reading a book, however, by Billy Graham called *The Secret of Happiness*. It was based on the Beatitudes. So I asked for a New Testament and began to read Matthew 5:1-12. Then I simply repeated whatever I remembered from Billy Graham's book.

As I was commenting on the Beatitude "Blessed are the pure in heart, for they shall see God," a lady suddenly stood up. She began to cry and said, "My heart is not pure. How can I see God? Somebody tell me how I can get a pure heart."

I don't remember the woman's name, but I will never forget her words, "Somebody tell me how I can get a pure heart." We went to the Bible and read, "The blood of Jesus, his [God's] Son, purifies us from all sin" (1 John 1:7). Before the evening was over, that woman found peace with God. She went home with a pure heart, overflowing with joy.

The greatest joy comes from winning people to Jesus Christ. Your graduation is exciting. Your wedding day is exciting. Your first baby is exciting. But the most thrilling thing you can ever do is win someone to Christ. And once you do it, you don't want to stop.

I challenge you to pray, "Oh, Lord, I want that experience. I want to know what it is to win someone to Jesus Christ."

Are you willing to gain a vision of what God could do through you to win others to Himself? After all, God doesn't have a Plan A, a Plan B and a Plan C for evangelizing the world. He has only one plan—and that's you and me. [5]

Notes
1. Charles B. Williams, trans., *The Williams New Testament* (Chicago, IL: Moody Publishers, 1972).
2. Ray Stedman, *From Guilt to Glory*, vol. 2 (Waco, TX: Word Books, 1978), p. 173.
3. From an article in *The Oregonian*, March 15, 1983.
4. "Financial Insider with Biblical Outlook," *Moody*, January 1995, p. 24.
5. This chapter is adapted from my "Dream Great Dreams" message, originally published in booklet form by Multnomah Press.

CHAPTER 4

PRIORITIZE TO EVANGELIZE

MINISTRY GOALS OF THE EVANGELIST

TIMOTHY ROBNETT

Luis Palau has often said, "My job as an evangelist is to stand at the door of the Kingdom and invite people in." It's true! Evangelists represent the Church and her mission in the public forum by communicating the truth of salvation. We are the primary harvesters of souls.

As evangelists, we are spokespersons for the Church, so we must be effective communicators. Just as we nurture our spiritual health, we must also cultivate our talents and gifts. We must continually evaluate our ability to clearly communicate the gospel, create and innovate new evangelistic methods, effectively lead our ministry team, and equip the Church for evangelism.

COMMUNICATE THE GOSPEL

Communication is the heartbeat of every evangelist, for if we do not effectively communicate the gospel message, we cannot expect anyone to make a life-changing decision based on our nebulous explanation. How do we achieve effective communication?

1. Be Authentic and Vulnerable

First, we must be authentic and vulnerable. This brings us back to the spiritual requirements of the evangelist: If the evangelist's personal relationship with God is not healthy, the audience will know it. Worse, the audience may be deceived or may misunderstand the message. Lack of authenticity breeds potential for miscommunication. Don't be afraid to speak from personal experience; in many ways, those vulnerable moments will be the key that unlocks a hardened heart.

2. Clearly Communicate the Good News

Different venues require different types of delivery. A one-on-one presentation of the gospel with a prison inmate requires a different type of language (verbal and nonverbal) than is required by a stadium-size gathering of 20,000 teenagers.

When Luis Palau's team coordinates a festival, the *Night Talk with Luis Palau* television show is often a part of the program. For an hour, Luis takes phone calls on live television to answer life's toughest questions. The set is designed as a comfortable home office, with Luis seated in business-casual clothing behind a warm mahogany desk. The callers' questions—and Luis's answers—are completely unprepared, so Luis engages in conversation with a Bible in his hand and the Spirit moving in his heart.

Luis does not employ the same method when he speaks at a large festival gathering. Because he is addressing a plethora of diverse personalities and a variety of needs, he prepares his message in advance. He also stands up before the crowd and roams the platform as he speaks, with a clear podium at center stage for his Bible, notes and water. Luis looks at the type of event to determine every facet of his communication style.

3. Always Center the Message on Jesus Christ

We may be the most engaging, dynamic and vulnerable speakers, but if our message is not centered on the truth of the gospel, every word will fall flat (or false). One of the best ways to ensure that our message is focused on the good news is to memorize Scripture.

One powerful way to memorize Scripture is to get to know the Bible's VIPs. When you study biblical figures, you will achieve greater understanding of the human heart. So familiarize yourself with the lives of Abraham, David, Jonah and the like. Discover the wisdom within their stories as you identify the major issues of the human soul and spirit. Biblical study will unlock not only a treasure trove of spiritual truth but also a vast library of psychological and sociological information.

4. Present an Invitation to Accept Christ

We must always present an invitation for people to accept Jesus Christ as their Lord and Savior. Revelation 22 emphasizes the word "come." Jesus says, "Come." The Spirit says, "Come." The Church says, "Come." When we present the gospel message, we, too, must say, "Come. Come to the living water who is Jesus Christ. Come today! Today is your day of salvation."

One of the most powerful invitations I have heard came from the mouth of evangelist Mike Silva. Gifted with the ability to use any object as an illustration for the gospel message, Mike used a flock of 50 goats in India to demonstrate the parable of the lost sheep. Roaming through the crowd with one goat slung across his shoulders, Mike clearly communicated God's search for the one lost sheep. He called for every lost individual in the crowd to come forward and be found by the risen Savior, Jesus Christ.[1]

Evangelists invite others into the Kingdom. That is where we are uniquely gifted to serve.

5. Know the Audience

The apostle Paul was a student of his time. He desired to know when and how to relate to a culture different from his own. In Acts 17, Paul travels to Athens and presents the gospel to this city of philosophers. As he speaks, we learn that Paul has studied the culture to better communicate the gospel message to his listeners: "Men of Athens! I see that in every way you are very religious. For as I walked around and looked carefully at your objects of worship, I even found an altar with this inscription: TO AN UNKNOWN GOD. Now what you worship as something unknown I am going to proclaim to you" (vv. 22-23).

Like Paul, we must ask questions and conduct research to identify the needs of every audience. Evangelist Steve Jamison has developed a focused ministry called Jammin' Against the Darkness. Because he is attempting to reach the youth that identify with basketball and the NBA, Steve has developed this outreach around basketball and fast-paced activities. For more than a decade, Steve has spoken to thousands of youth who, through their excitement about basketball, faced the darkness of their lost souls with a new sense of hope.[2]

Hollywood thrives on communicating the latest social themes and on setting trends for the youth of America. Using the latest movie to illustrate our need for Jesus and the good news can capture the attention of your audience. So what's the latest illustration that you could use to spread the message?

CREATE AND INNOVATE

Picture this: You have just returned home from a long day of work with your ministry team. Looking for a bit of relaxation, you collapse onto the couch and flip on the television set. After just a few minutes, you straighten up and stare at the screen in confusion. Why have the past three commercials advertised typewriters, station wagons and rotary phones? This is the beginning of the twenty-first century! Where are all the commercials for personal computers, SUVs, cellular phones and iPods?

You see, without innovation, the business world would come to a standstill. As society changes, businesses tailor products and advertising to accommodate those changes. We must do the same with evangelism.

Sterling Huston presents a great example of innovative evangelism. For three decades, Sterling served the Billy Graham Evangelistic Association (BGEA) with great success as a crusade director. But several years ago, he realized that the Internet offers a great new way to communicate the good news of Jesus Christ. Today, Sterling directs BGEA's thriving Internet ministry, with a home page posted in 11 languages, *Decision* magazine online, and the passageway.org youth website, which is visited daily by thousands of teenagers.

Kevin Palau and Hollywood notable Stephen Baldwin have teamed up to create the latest Luis Palau Association ministry, called Livin It. This extreme-sports ministry focuses on the athletic abilities of skateboarders and BMX riders to capture the attention of thousands of youth across America. Along with a national tour, the Livin It ministry has created two edgy DVDs, *Livin It* and *Livin It LA*. These reality-type productions have proven extremely popular with the younger crowds. New generations need new approaches to communicate the good news of Jesus.

Effective evangelism requires that old methods be retooled with new approaches. Like D. L. Moody, Sterling Huston, and Kevin Palau and Stephen Baldwin, we must constantly seek out new and creative ways to present the gospel message. Innovation requires risk, and that can be fearsome. When we introduce a new avenue for reaching the lost, we may not see immediate results. But those evangelists who base their identity in godly leadership and wisdom will consistently evaluate ministry methodology and prayerfully make the changes that will reap a harvest in the long run.

BUILD YOUR TEAM

I'm sure you've heard the axiom, "Together Everyone Achieves More." Its acronym, TEAM, denotes an essential component of effective evangelistic ministry. Just as the Body of Christ requires many parts to function, so our ministry team finds success in a variety of team members with different skills and gifts. We cannot fulfill the Great Commission alone.

To facilitate a thriving ministry, an evangelist should consider three unique teams:

1. **Prayer Team.** Paul told Timothy that the first priority of ministry is prayer: "I urge, then, first of all, that requests, prayers, intercession and thanksgiving be made for everyone" (1 Tim. 2:1-4). Evangelists must pray for their ministry and recruit as many devoted prayer warriors as possible. Remember that your team includes everyone who participates in your ministry, from hired employees

to financial supporters to friends and family. Recruit from these groups, and have your people focus their prayer time on specific items of praise and need. Keep your prayer team updated on answered prayers and additional requests, and don't forget to pray for your prayer warriors.

You may also consider holding regular prayer retreats for your ministry or bringing a prayer team with you to evangelistic events. When NGA emerging evangelist Reid Saunders went to Madurai, India, he brought prayer warrior Mike McCarthy with him. As rain fell from the clouds and umbrellas rose into the sky, Mike stood before the crowd and rebuked the weather in the name of Jesus Christ. A few minutes later, the rain stopped, the umbrellas came down, and Reid took the stage to preach the gospel message.

2. **Board of Directors / Senior Advisors.** "Plans fail for lack of counsel, but with many advisers they succeed" (Prov. 15:22). Ministry success comes when we rely on the wisdom of a council of advisors. Look to this group to discuss big-ticket ministry items such as your vision and mission statement, strategic planning, and your budget. Think seriously—and pray faithfully—over the selection of these counselors. Ask yourself the following questions: Is this a godly person with an obvious passion for evangelism? Will this person bring experience beyond my own knowledge? Will this person help identify potential ministry dangers? Will this person help protect me (and the ministry) from burning out?

3. **Ministry Team.** "Brothers, choose seven men from among you who are known to be full of the Spirit and wisdom. We will turn this responsibility over to them"

(Acts 6:3). When the number of disciples was increasing but the number of apostles wasn't, the Twelve gathered together and decided to recruit some help. Like the apostles, long-time evangelist Luis Palau did not start with a large and established ministry team, but eventually his team needed to grow into a structure of departments and vice presidents.

Don't expect huge growth in the early stages of your ministry. Find three to five people to serve with you, with each individual bringing a different set of complementary gifts to the team. Make sure you have someone with business savvy to address the legalities of operating a nonprofit organization. Find someone with experience in fund-raising to help sustain the ministry's financial livelihood. And, of course, pray that God will bring you someone (or two) with the gift of event leadership. Although in the beginning you may participate significantly in planning an event, you will need someone to care for the details on the day of the event.

Of course, none of these teams will experience healthy growth without a strong leader. Only as evangelists cultivate leadership skills will they effectively guide their teams. No matter how long you serve as an evangelist and a team leader, you must continually educate yourself in successful leadership. Read books, attend seminars, and communicate with other leaders. Maintain a mentor relationship with an older, more experienced evangelist, as we discussed in chapter 2. Always feed into relationships with your ministry teams so that they become comfortable in keeping you accountable to your role as leader.

Above all else, remember the following four tips on effective leadership:

1. Trust Your Team

If you follow this first guideline, I assure you that the next three will be easy to follow. If you doubt a team member's character, skills or competence, then it is easy to undermine his or her work. When you trust someone, it is easier to surrender some control to him or her, have confidence in the results, and ask that person for feedback when you are making an important decision.

But trust does not stop there. To trust a team member means that you speak well of that person in public. Luis Palau does so by honoring festival directors in each city in front of that city's leaders and the press. True, you may not have city leaders listening to your message, much less your praise, as you begin an evangelistic ministry. For now, public praise can be as simple as an encouraging word within earshot of fellow coworkers.

Trust also means respecting a team member's sense of honor and need for privacy. If a confrontation is required, it should always be done in private and with a spirit of humility.

2. Delegate Responsibilities

As you begin an evangelistic ministry, you may do a lot of the behind-the-scenes work yourself. But as your ministry grows, it will become necessary to develop a team of people with gifting in different areas of ministry.

When you ask someone to write a support letter, sign a contract for services provided to the team, or negotiate dates or venues for an evangelistic event, trust that person to successfully complete the task, even when he or she takes an approach different from one you might choose. Evangelists who do not learn to give away many of the "jobs" of the ministry will become a stumbling block to their ministry's growth.

Above all else, you must remember that there is nothing quite as devastating to a team member as having a delegated task taken back by the "boss." Consider carefully the circumstances in which you take back a task and be sure that you have covered your decision with much thought and prayer. Remember that your team will endure growing pains. These will not be the times to take back the job, but to evaluate and encourage your team members to grow from the experience.

3. Encourage All the Time

When you select team members with specific ministry gifting and an obvious passion for evangelism, you will see in these people a desire to succeed and to please you as the leader of the ministry. But life is difficult, and problems arise every day.

To overcome these hurdles, the evangelist must be a Barnabas to his team members. How? With words of encouragement. When discussing trust, we recognized the importance of public honor. But encouragement does not have to be given on a large scale. A note of encouragement or a small reward can lift almost anyone's spirit.

When you do need to criticize a team member's performance, keep this ratio in mind: For every word of criticism, the evangelist needs to speak *five to seven* messages of encouragement. And don't forget that one of life's easiest encouragements—saying "thank you"—can inspire immeasurable outcomes.

4. Resist Micromanagement

You may have mastered the task of not taking back a delegated responsibility, but you are still at risk for one of the greatest leadership mistakes of all time: micromanagement. Nothing can be more discouraging (and often destructive) than an evangelist going behind a team member's back to get his or her way.

If you have delegated a task to be completed in a specified amount of time, step away from the responsibility and trust your team member to successfully complete the task without your eyes boring holes into the back of his or her head. There is a time and place for feedback, but that time is not in the middle of a project when your advice is unsolicited.

When evangelists give and then take back a task or job, they are communicating lack of trust and respect to their team members.

When you trust a team member with a delegated responsibility and provide ongoing encouragement without micromanagement, your team will flourish under your umbrella of trust and respect.

EQUIP THE CHURCH

As evangelists, we have a twofold responsibility to the Body of Christ. First, we must encourage and motivate people to fulfill the Great Commission in their families, neighborhoods and workplaces. Second, we must equip those individuals with the tools necessary to communicate the good news. Other gifted leaders can equip the Church for evangelistic ministry, but I believe evangelists do it with unique empowerment from the Holy Spirit.

Over the past 15 years, I have been privileged to witness two of the most powerful components of Luis Palau's ministry designed to empower the Church: friendship evangelism training and counselor training.

By using gifted evangelists to lead these training courses, people learn from the best of the best. The evangelist's motivation is contagious. His or her enthusiasm infects the most hesitant soul. People leave the training courses energized in their faith and confident in their ability to fulfill the Great Commission. They are excited to share Jesus Christ in word and deed with those God has placed in their sphere of influence.

By training the Church to present the life-changing gospel of Jesus Christ, we reap a greater harvest before, during and after public evangelistic events.

Notes

1. Mike Silva, *Would You Like Fries with That?* (Nashville, TN: World Publishing, 2005), n.p.
2. For more information, visit the Jammin' Against the Darkness website at http://www.jamminevents.org.

CHAPTER 5

PROCLAIM GOOD NEWS

THE MESSAGE OF THE EVANGELIST

LUIS PALAU

The impact of the good news about Jesus Christ is mighty and powerful. But what is the essence of the gospel message? This chapter is going to take a look at what we, as evangelists, should be preaching.

Are you crazy? you might be thinking. *Do we really have to go over that?* Yes, we do. I've been to dozens of Billy Graham conferences, and every time, he starts out by asking, "What is the gospel?" He admits that it seems embarrassing, in a congress of evangelists, that we have to go over the content of the gospel again each time. But it has to be done.

Too many people get confused by the question, "What is the gospel?" and, on the other hand, "What isn't the gospel?"

In our campaigns, we use the phrase "good news gospel." The word "gospel" in English means nothing. It's not an English word, and therefore English-speaking people who are not believers don't know what in the world we're talking about.

It would make the members of the Church much more comfortable sharing about Jesus if they saw it as *good news*. When you say "gospel," if you're like me, you think of a certain package, the gospel—basic truths—and you feel nervous because you think you won't be able to answer all the questions that might be asked about it. But *good news* is another story. Good news is saying, "I've got a free ticket to heaven. Do you want to hear about it?"

We evangelists live to proclaim *good news*. And the good news is that God sent His Son, Jesus Christ, who was born of the Virgin Mary, lived a holy life, died on a cross, gave His blood, was buried, rose from the dead, ascended to heaven, and is waiting to come back. The good news is that all you have to do, if you truly know and acknowledge that you're guilty, is to believe, repent and receive Jesus Christ by faith. That is the essence of the good news.

WHAT IS SO GOOD ABOUT THE GOOD NEWS?

This essence of the gospel is found in John 3:16-17: "For God so loved the world that he gave his one and only Son, that whoever believes in him shall not perish but have eternal life. For God did not send his Son into the world to condemn the world, but to save the world through him."

That's what Jesus came to do. The good news is centered on the person and work of Jesus Christ: "That Christ died for our sins according to the Scriptures, that he was buried, and that he was raised on the third day" (1 Cor. 15:3-4).

Evangelism is the communication of that message. If you're an evangelist—whether it's one on one, door to door, in small groups, at camp, in Sunday School or through major festivals—you are a communicator of the good news of Jesus Christ. That is what an evangelist is really all about. You may do other things in connection with it, but you're only being an evangelist when you clearly communicate the content of the gospel—the good news of Jesus, the person of Christ and the work of Christ—and when you call people to believe, repent and receive Jesus Christ.

The Good News of God's Power

"I am not ashamed of the gospel, because it is the power of God for the salvation of everyone who believes" (Rom. 1:16). The power is the message, not the messenger. The truth has power, and when you present the truth, the Lord will use it. What converts people is the truth.

The Good News of God's Love

God is a good God. Many people don't believe this. Even in the Church, people get nervous about this. In some theological seminaries, professors get quite worked up about this. "Don't keep saying that God is a good God, because then they'll all want to be converted! Don't tell them God is a good God, or they might actually believe it."

Sadly, that's why many churches never grow. I was brought up in churches where the preacher spent 55 minutes blasting the sinners and only briefly on offering forgiveness and eternal life. The feeling was that if people weren't on their knees crying and beating their breasts, they weren't truly converted.

But Jesus said to go into *all* the world and preach the good news. It's *good* news because God is a good God who loves people.

The Good News of God's Self-Sacrifice

God is a forgiving God. Jesus Christ was our substitute on the cross of Calvary. You aren't preaching the good news if you don't preach the substitutionary death of Christ. Of course, don't overuse that word, because even people in the Church often won't know what you're talking about. But it is crucial that we explain that Christ died in our place and use His story to illustrate that fact.

The Good News of the Living God

In 1 Thessalonians 1:9, Paul commends the Thessalonian church for turning from idols to serve the living God. A conversion takes place.

The word "conversion" can be a turnoff to some people. Conversion implies, "You want me to stop being Baptist and become Presbyterian, is that it?" Or, "I was born a Methodist, and now you want me to become something else. What's my mother-in-law going to say? She's going to cut me out of her will."

During a campaign in Nepal, I opened my remarks by saying, "I am not here to get you to leave Hinduism and become a Christian. I'm here to tell you about Jesus, who is the most wonderful man you'll ever meet. I want to help you fall in love with Him, receive Him into your life, and follow Him."

Now, I know that when people meet Jesus, fall in love with Him, and surrender their lives to Him, certain events will follow. But I am not there to turn people from Hinduism to Christianity. I want them to turn from sin to Jesus, from lostness to eternal life. Everything else will happen later.

The man who led my grandmother, mother, dad, all my sisters and me to Jesus Christ presented the good news. My mother was the organist at the local parish church, and after she was converted, she asked our missionary, "Should I stop playing the organ at the Catholic parish?"

"No," he said. "Keep playing, but on Sunday nights come to Bible study, and just don't worry about it." Within a year, after reading the Bible and listening at the Bible studies, my mother joined the tiny local church's community of believers. Nobody told her to do so—she just chose to do it.

My grandmother, before she was converted, promised one of the saints that if her son was not forced to join the military, every year she would walk on her knees two kilometers to the shrine. After she received Jesus Christ, she couldn't stop. She said, "I made a promise, and a promise is a promise. My son did not go to the military service. Yes, I received Jesus Christ as my only Savior, but I'm going to keep my promise every year and walk on my knees to the shrine."

My grandmother did this for three years. The fourth year, my mother was expecting her to go again, but instead she said, "You know, it's a waste of time. The saint couldn't hear my prayers." Nobody told her this—she just came to realize it from personal prayer and Bible study.

I grew up not with a hatred of Roman Catholics but with a love and compassion for them. That, I think, has confounded many Roman Catholic leaders who thought I was coming to steal their people. I'm not interested in stealing any Catholics to become dead Protestants. We want people to come alive to God through Jesus Christ and then join the living Church.

The Good News of a Personal God
Not only is God living, but He's also personal. In John 14, Jesus uses the word "Father" more than 20 times to describe God. God wants to know us intimately.

I thank God for the missionaries who came to Latin America when I was young. They brought nothing but the Bible and the good news—that was it. No schools, no seminaries, no hospitals—they just wanted us to go to heaven when we died. The rest was up to us and the power of the Holy Spirit. They gave us the good news.

Amazing things have happened in Latin America as a result. The missionaries didn't bring us rice and hospitals and other stuff. They brought us Jesus. And Jesus changed our lives.

The Good News of Happiness

I once did an interview in England with a man named Joe. During our interview, he asked, "Mr. Palau, have you ever been to one of our Anglican churches?"

"Yes, I have," I replied.

"Have you ever looked at the faces of people?"

"Usually I see the back of their heads, but sometimes if I'm preaching, then yes, I see them."

"Have you ever seen one of them that looks happy?"

"Some do."

He asked, "Why should I go and listen to a group of people who sit there looking glum and miserable and unfriendly?"

Sadly, many people feel just like Joe, and I can't blame them. Why can't we truly be ourselves? The good news *is* good news of happiness. The angel said to the shepherds, "I bring you good news of great joy that will be for all the people" (Luke 2:10).

We are called to proclaim good news. Never forget that. This is the privilege of being an evangelist. Some people say an evangelist must preach the whole counsel of God. If you're a preacher, then yes, the people of the Church need to learn all about the Bible. But an evangelist is not there to give the whole counsel of God—an evangelist doesn't have time. He or she is there to present the good news of forgiveness, eternal life, and the assurance that those who believe are forever children of God.

Over and over, the Bible talks about joy. Jesus wants His people to be happy. But unfortunately, we often give the impression that happiness is an abnormal state. As sons and daughters of the King, we should be the most joyful people in the world—and others should see that!

The Good News of Eternal Life Assured

John 10:28 says, "I give them eternal life, and they shall never perish; no one can snatch them out of my hand." The good news gives people the hope of eternal life.

One of the great things about preaching the good news in the Third World is that people are more humble. Many are uneducated, don't have much money, and live simple lives—but when they meet Jesus Christ, they come alive.

Rosario Rivera is a former guerrilla fighter whom I met about 12 years after she was saved. I had heard how she had changed. She had been a wild woman, born out of wedlock, living in the slums outside of Lima, Peru. She had been an active atheistic Marxist-Leninist, had children out of wedlock, and had killed 12 people. She had come to Lima to recruit more fighters, but instead she was converted during one of our early campaigns. Her life was radically changed through Jesus Christ. She started preaching the good news!

When I finally had the chance to meet Rosario, she talked to me about a biblical worldview, about governments, about truth and evil, and I was completely amazed. Here was a woman who had almost no education, who had come out of complete paganism, and she had a biblical view of the world and of God's sovereignty and of justice and truth and freedom that was amazing. You would have thought that she had been brought up in a Christian home with a preacher father who knew the Bible.

The good news is the tremendous life of God in the soul of man. It's an astonishing thing.

GOOD NEWS VS. GOOD ADVICE

You would be amazed how many people confuse other good, healthy and even biblical teachings with the basic, clear, good news. We can talk about being a loving husband or a good wife or obeying one's parents, but that's not the gospel. That's teaching on the family.

Preaching sexual self-control is vital; it's the will of God and saves you from a million troubles, but it's not in itself the good news. Education and intellectual attainments are vital for success; Greek word studies and gaining wisdom are excellent, but that's not the gospel.

You can stand up and preach and get cheap applause by attacking certain sins or mocking certain lifestyles that irritate you, but that isn't the good news; it's usually more an expression of an angry heart than a loving communication of God's salvation message about Jesus Christ. Discussions on topics such as those may have their place, but when it comes to sharing the good news, Jesus Christ is the focus—nothing else.

We're supposed to proclaim the good news. God is alive, knows each of us, and wants us. Once people receive Jesus Christ, if they really have the love of God in them, then they will stop worshiping idols, getting drunk, committing immorality, or whatever other sin God has convicted them of. You can blast sinners all you want, but it will have little effect without the indwelling power of the Holy Spirit.

Don't get me wrong. A pastor does need to take a stance on sin issues. The job of a pastor is to teach the whole counsel of God. But as an evangelist, when you only have 30 or 40 minutes in front of a crowd or with a neighbor, wouldn't you rather spend that time sharing the good news of Jesus' love and His work on the cross?

God is not an angry God. We may be angry, but we should never impose our personal feelings on the way we present God. God is not an angry God, and we are not called to portray Him as such. That's not the gospel. You need to be part of the good-news team. When you and your team show up to share the good news, Christians and non-Christians alike should say, "Here comes the good-news team!" People are sick and tired of bad news. They get enough of that from the newspapers and the evening news.

We had a statewide mission in Maine a few years ago, and as I sat waiting for the press conference to begin, I thought, *Lord I'm not satisfied with the stuff I've been saying in press conferences. Give me something fresh.* And I felt the Lord saying to me, *Make it as simple as you can.*

I thought about the reason I came to Christ. I wanted to go to heaven when I died, and I wanted to have the absolute assurance my dad had when he died. He was singing and quoting the apostle Paul, "I am going to be with Jesus, which is much better" (see Phil. 1:23). I wanted to see my dad. Maybe I had the wrong motives, but I wanted to be saved—and I was, at 12 years old.

So at the press conference I said, "I want every person in Maine to go to heaven when they die, because that's what God wants. God wants all men to be saved and to come to the knowledge of the truth," which is exactly what we read in 1 Timothy 2:4.

Peter writes that God "is patient . . . not wanting anyone to perish, but everyone to come to repentance" (2 Pet. 3:9). God's desire is that every human come to eternal life. Anybody who says otherwise is contradicting the clear content of Scripture. God wants *all* people.

When you get up to share the good news, don't hold back. No matter how you feel about your neighbor, coworker, brother or father, realize that God loves them and wants them to be saved. God loves the people of the world, and He wants them to believe, repent and receive Jesus Christ.

Don't forget that you are a proclaimer of good news. "But what about the bad news?" you might ask. Leave that to the Holy Spirit. John 16:8 says that "he will convict the world of guilt in regard to sin and righteousness and judgment." We have been sent out to proclaim the good news. We have not been sent out to convict the world of sin, righteousness and judgment. That is the work of the

Holy Spirit, and the third person of the blessed trinity is constantly at His convicting work.

Of course, some servants of God are called to be prophets. They denounce sin, particularly in the Church, the house of God. Prophets are called to point the finger. But be careful—prophets very often lose their heads. I'm glad that I was called to be an evangelist, not a prophet. We evangelists preach the good news that "everyone who believes in [God] will not perish but have everlasting life" (John 3:16).

Imagine that someone has given you tickets to go see your favorite football team play and two hundred dollars to go to dinner afterward. But your kids don't want to go. So you go to your neighbor apologetically and say, "I hate to bother you, but I know you love the Seattle Seahawks, and I have some extra tickets. But I'm embarrassed to offer them to you, because you might feel bad about it. And I also have two hundred dollars for you to go to dinner. You don't really want to come, do you? No, you probably don't."

No way! You say, "Hey, man! I've got six tickets—let's go see the Seahawks and go out to dinner!" because you have good news to share.

Become a member of the good-news team. When others talk to you, let them see the good news. Often, people are already convicted of sin. Why do you think unbelievers come to an evangelistic campaign? Because they have nothing better to do? No, it's because the Holy Spirit draws them. He's convicting them, and He sets them before you, saying, in a way, "Look, I could do this without you, but I'm going to give you the privilege of giving them My good news. Now do it!"

Your job is to tell people the good news as best you can. As mass evangelists, we have the privilege of simply showing up in town to give good news—there's hardly a better deal in the world. In Philemon 6, Paul writes, "I pray that you may be active in sharing your faith, so that you will have a full understanding of every good thing we have in Christ."

Don't forget to preach the gospel on the basis of the Second Coming. That's part of the good news—Christ is coming back. You don't need to get into the details, but share the basic concept of the Second Coming of our Lord and Savior, Jesus Christ. What are you waiting for next in God's agenda of world events? I'm waiting for the Son to show up in the clouds in the twinkling of an eye with the trumpet sounding (see John 14:1-6; 1 Thess. 4:13-17).

THE EVANGELISTIC MESSAGE

Now that you know *what* you're preaching, here are a few specific things to remember as you craft your evangelistic message.

An evangelistic sermon, if based on the Word of God and anointed by the Holy Spirit, can effect the greatest possible life change. In the sovereignty of God, your words can speak to an unbeliever and turn his or her heart to faith in Jesus Christ. Let's consider seven aspects of an effective evangelistic sermon.

1. Topic

Choosing a specific topic and developing it usually works best, whether the topic is God Himself, loneliness, forgiveness, freedom, peace, purity, happiness, heaven, or true Christianity. The chosen topic should interest the listeners and relate to their situation. As we speak, our teaching should go from what the listeners know to what they don't know, from what they're looking for to what they're not looking for but need.

You're free to use your imagination and creativity when trying to communicate the message of salvation. Look at the example the apostle Paul provides. As explained in 1 Corinthians 9:19-22, Paul would adapt his presentation of the gospel to whatever situation he was in. When he wanted to lead a Jew to Christ, he talked about topics of relevance to the Jewish way of thinking. When he talked to the Gentiles, he became like a Gentile.

Remarkably, Paul could adapt his message to reach any and every audience. In one week, he could preach in the Jewish synagogue (see Acts 17:17a), in the marketplace (see Acts 17:17b), and then to the intelligentsia of Athens (see Acts 17:18-31). His sermon to the Areopagus demonstrates our need to target our presentation of the same gospel message to the specific groups before us.

2. Message

While the announced topic of an evangelistic message may not be necessarily sacred, the message itself is, and it can't be changed or tampered with. The core of any evangelistic sermon has to be Jesus Christ's work on the cross. Otherwise, the message ignores the gospel and is not evangelistic.

The heart, the backbone, of any evangelistic message can be summarized this way: "That Christ died for our sins according to the Scriptures, that he was buried, that he was raised on the third day according to the Scriptures" (1 Cor. 15:3-4). Or it can be compressed even further into what some have called the miniature gospel: "God so loved the world that he gave his one and only Son" (John 3:16). Saturate people with these gospel truths, which can be planted in their hearts and minds by the Holy Spirit and can bear fruit for eternity.

3. Language

It's crucial to preach an evangelistic sermon in simple, understandable terms. A profound theological dissertation or word study may be great for those already part of God's eternal kingdom, but for those who are not, we need to speak in simple terms, not evangelical jargon. Biblical terms like "regeneration," "redemption" and "justification" need contemporary equivalents, without diminishing their depth of meaning. As I said, nobody even knows what "gospel" means anymore. Simplify difficult terms so that all listeners can understand your message.

4. Illustrations

An effective communicator uses contemporary examples and anecdotes. This helps keep listeners attentive. If at all possible, use illustrations from everyday life. Billy Graham often quotes from newspapers, citing events and personalities of the day, to highlight the urgency and relevance of his message.

5. Focus

An evangelistic sermon shouldn't be used as a platform to change the audience's political viewpoint. Your objective is to win hearts to God. The message of good news is for the whole world. Your message must center on Jesus Christ and proclaim that Jesus, the sinless Son of God, died for our sins, rose from the dead, is alive, and is coming again. Everyone who believes this message, regardless of his or her past or political persuasion, inherits eternal life. We can't afford to preach *against* this or that issue. Rather, let's preach *for* Christ, proclaiming the good news of eternal life in a positive way, with power from above.

6. Structure

As with other types of sermons, the evangelistic message needs to hang on a logical structure. The overall objective, of course, is to call people in the audience to decide for Christ. As noted above, the theme can vary depending on which topic interests your audience.

The *introduction* to your message must capture the attention of your listeners within the first few phrases. If you start an evangelistic sermon in a predictable manner, your audience won't hear you out. If, on the other hand, your opening remarks are compelling, you will have hooked your audience, and they'll listen to the central part of your message.

Ideally, the *body* of an evangelistic message should have only three or four main points to make it easier for the audience to remember them. I'm afraid I break this principle too often, and I visibly pay for it.

The *conclusion* of an evangelistic sermon should lead to a climax that confronts listeners with the need to make a decision before the claims of Christ. At that climactic moment, the preacher—who is God's voice and mouth (see Jer. 15:19; 1 Pet. 4:11)—should ask listeners to repent and believe the truth that has just been proclaimed. By "climax," I don't necessarily mean something emotional, but rather something spiritual that engages the listeners at every level of their being—intellect, emotions and will. Without a call to commitment, an evangelistic sermon is dysfunctional.

Jesus Himself demanded that people make a decision about Him (see Matt. 4:19; John 3:36). Make your listeners see they're at a crossroad. Preach in such a way that unbelievers face a dilemma and must ask, "What am I going to do with Christ?"

IMPORTANCE OF THE INVITATION

When I was young, my pastor preached the good news of salvation in a theological, doctrinal and biblical way. I thank God for that church. But there was one problem: Practically no one was being converted; the church wasn't growing. Whenever one person trusted Christ, it felt like a revival. How sad, after the gospel was preached so accurately, that nobody trusted Christ!

The heart of the matter was that we had instructive evangelism instead of decisive evangelism. The preaching of the gospel should go hand in hand with an invitation for the listener to believe, surrender, receive Christ and trust Him for salvation. Without an invitation, you are not preaching the full good news of Jesus Christ.

Some preachers exclude invitations to trust Christ from their sermons because they don't want to offend anyone or make them feel uncomfortable. Others give no clear-cut call to commitment because they're afraid that if no one makes a public stand for Christ, they will have failed. (Far from it!) Still other preachers believe salvation is solely God's responsibility, so they don't try to persuade anyone to trust Christ. How different this is from the approach of the apostles Peter (see Acts 2:44-46) and Paul (see 2 Cor. 5:11-13)!

I'm not suggesting we should give an overly emotive appeal. Nor am I saying we have to give a lengthy or negative invitation, obligating someone to respond and shaming the unconverted by manipulation and glib techniques. But if we're afraid we'll offend someone by giving an invitation, our blossoming evangelistic efforts will never reach fruition.

If you want to preach an evangelistic message that yields fruit, give people an opportunity to make a commitment to Jesus Christ. In Revelation 3:20, Jesus says, "Here I am! I stand at the door and knock. If anyone hears my voice and opens the door, I will come in and eat with him, and he with me." On many occasions Jesus gave His listeners a clear opportunity to make a choice between surrender or rebellion, light or darkness, hope or despair. So should we.

As we communicate the message and give an invitation, we need to confront unbelievers as Jesus did, in a compassionate and loving way (see Mark 10:21), so that they won't close their ears or heart to God's voice. I find that people want to know what steps to take to respond to Christ. Ours is the pleasure of telling them quite specifically and simply.

My insistence on giving an invitation is borne out not only by Scripture but also by experience. My mother admitted, "I had been on the verge of receiving Christ many times, but I didn't do it because the preacher wouldn't give me the chance." Give an invitation to receive Christ every time you preach the gospel. Remember, it might be somebody's last chance to receive the Lord.

Do you preach a gospel that demands a decision? Or do you preach a message so diluted that people leave with the feeling you are nothing more than a friendly communicator?

So much still needs to be done to win the world for Christ. How long will people in our congregations and communities have to wait until they are given a chance to respond to the gospel? Are we willing to show compassion and try urgently to win the lost to Christ?

CHAPTER 6

What If I'm Not an Itinerant?

Ministry Positions for an Evangelist in the Twenty-First Century

Timothy Robnett

Do all evangelists fulfill the same ministry positions? Are all evangelists, like Moody, Graham or Palau, conducting large mass meetings?

The young evangelist must ask several key questions: Where will I begin? How can I fulfill my calling to preach the gospel? What can I do to cultivate a lifetime of meaningful service for the Lord in the harvest?

There is not one single pathway to fulfilling your call as an evangelist. History has demonstrated that people start at many different places, yet along the journey of life they find unique and powerful ways of winning people to Christ. Luis Palau preached as a young man working with his church in Argentina. After formal training at Multnomah Biblical Seminary, Luis and Pat Palau served with Overseas Crusades as missionaries to South America. Within 15 years of beginning this mission work, Luis became the president of Overseas Crusades. Yet this was not a long-term role. Luis was compelled to focus on preaching internationally to large audiences. His role as president of a missions organization, though noble, was not where he was to see the greatest impact of his ministry.

God calls each of us to a different aspect of evangelism. All Christians are witnesses—but some of us have a special passion to see thousands come to Christ. However, even among evangelists, there will be some who see a harvest of thirtyfold, others who see sixtyfold, and others who see a hundredfold. Just like in the parable of the sower (see Matt. 13), there will be a variety of outcomes, but they will all honor God.

Try to discern from God what kind of evangelist He wants you to be. Not everyone can be a Billy Graham. If that's your only dream, you're going to be sorely disappointed. Instead, ask God to affirm if you're to be an evangelist to university students, or an evangelist to prisoners in jail, or an evangelist in some other position. There are endless possibilities for the person who has a heart ready to serve God.

ROLES OF THE EVANGELIST IN THE WORLDWIDE CHURCH

The evangelist, I believe, has several strategic purposes within the Body of Christ. These purposes are expressed in a variety of ministry roles working with, through and for the Church of Jesus Christ. First, let's look at the primary roles of the evangelist in the life of the Church worldwide.

Communicator of the Gospel

The evangelist is a communicator of the gospel for the Church and the primary harvester of souls. As preachers of the good news, evangelists represent the Church and her mission in a public forum.

The evangelist's first role, then, is to preach the story of Jesus the Christ and what it means to know Him as Savior and Lord. The evangelist invites, encourages and implores people to open their hearts to Christ. A unique sense of timing and urgency mark the evangelist. The evangelist is also an inviter: "Today is the day of salvation" marks the conclusion of the evangelistic message. The evangelist used by the Holy Spirit welcomes people into the family of God.

Seeker of Souls

The second role of the evangelist is to be a seeker of souls. The heart of the evangelist is consumed with the need to win lost souls. Whether we emotionally identify with this idea or not, an evangelist must always be consumed by the need for those without Christ to come into a relationship with Him.

Evangelists will often be too bold and confrontational for the "typical" Christian. In February 2002, Brad Butcher, a Multnomah Biblical Seminary student working with Next Generation Alliance, preached at a four-day festival in Kariapotti, Tamil Nadu, India. As his professor, I attended one of the evenings with him and his brother Brett. I was encouraged to see Brad's joy and boldness as he walked up and down the main street of that city, engaging people with a friendly smile and inviting them to the Good News Festival. Brad was so concerned about the people, whose language he did not speak but whose souls he desired to introduce to Jesus Christ, that he went out into the streets to compel them to come to the meetings. Brad's boldness, I believe, stems from his passion for the lost. Evangelists have a unique and overwhelming passion for those in spiritual darkness. Their compassion empowers them to act in intentional ways to bring these people to Christ.

Equipper for Personal Evangelism

Evangelists also have a unique role in equipping Christians for personal evangelism. Dr. Bill Bright, founder of Campus Crusade for Christ, taught tens of thousands of Christians how to share the gospel through the Four Spiritual Laws. Evangelists equip the Church not just in the "how to" of evangelism, but also through the Spirit of Christ who uses evangelists to motivate believers to pray and speak for Christ.

Evangelists need to be positioned by Church leaders to train and teach believers in personal evangelism, new methods of evangelism, apologetics, understanding the culture of the day, and other topics that mobilize the Church in evangelistic ministry. Yes, other gifted leaders can equip the Church for ministry, but evangelists do so with unique empowerment from the Holy Spirit, bringing greater involvement by the Church in evangelistic witness.

Motivator of the Church

Fourth, evangelists are special motivators of the Church. Their gifting by the Spirit of Christ manifests itself in their ability to energize other believers to participate in the work of evangelism. There is a unique energy when evangelists are given the opportunity to train other believers. If we want empowerment and not just information and technique, we will position called and gifted evangelists to equip the Church through biblical training in evangelism.

Innovator of New Ministries

A fifth role for the evangelist in the life of the Church is that of an innovator of new ministries.

D. L. Moody used the invention of the light bulb and electricity to capture the attention of thousands of people in Chicago. Moody's church was destroyed in the great Chicago fire of 1871, and when the new auditorium was built, Moody insisted that electrical wiring be used in constructing the new auditorium so that lights could be installed. This allowed the Moody Church to conduct meetings at night—a novelty at the time. A new method of using the latest technology was introduced for evangelistic purposes.

David Jones, vice president of administration for the Luis Palau Evangelistic Association, informed our cabinet members in the fall of 2005 that 90 percent of our ministry had changed in the past seven years. Why? Because evangelists are innovative, which our changing world demands. The Palau Association festival model, Next Generation Alliance, and Livin It have all been created and implemented in just a brief period of time. Innovate or become obsolete!

Statesmen for Christ

Some evangelists have become statesman for Christ. Billy Graham stands out in our generation as one who is highly regarded by the masses and fulfills the role of a Christian statesman. Political and civic leaders look up to those who demonstrate integrity. When crisis comes, these individuals are often called upon to make statements to the community at large.

Evangelists can fulfill this role with power and great influence. Unfortunately, evangelists can also discredit the gospel and Christ by leading immoral lives, as we have sadly seen in America over the past three decades. But evangelists who walk with God in holiness can have a powerful and positive impact.

Steve Wingfield provided statesmanlike leadership for his hometown of Harrisonburg, Virginia, just days after Hurricane Katrina devastated the Gulf Coast of the United States in September 2005. Because of his integrity and credibility as an evangelist and leader in his hometown, he was able to call the city to action in a matter of days, providing an exceptional amount of aid for the storm-torn region of Mississippi. Because of Steve's maturity and effectiveness in evangelizing his own city, the civic, religious and business leaders were willing to listen to his voice and follow his leadership. Evangelists can win the right to be statesmen for their cities, states and nations.

Leader of Leaders

Finally, some evangelists will be a leader of leaders in the Church of Jesus Christ. Bill Hybels stands out to me as an evangelist who serves as a leader of leaders in the American Church. Willow Creek Church and all those associated with its purpose and vision are unquestionably evangelistic. They study evangelism. They structure themselves to reach the unsaved. Their whole mind-set is on winning those without Christ, and their method of ministry has been formed around the question, "How can we reach those who are lost?" They have fulfilled their ministry with great passion, commitment and excellence. Scores of other churches, denominations and Christian schools look to Willow Creek as a model of ministry in the twenty-first century. Evangelists can influence a whole generation of Christian leaders by working passionately with intelligence, love and endurance.

MINISTRY POSITIONS FOR TODAY'S EVANGELIST

The evangelist can fulfill these roles in the Church through a variety of ministry positions. What are these positions, and where can evangelists serve the Church with power and excellence? Let's now consider some ministry positions for today's evangelist.

Itinerant Evangelist

The most obvious to me is the itinerant evangelist. Billy Graham, Luis Palau, Steve Wingfield, Mike Silva and Jose Zayas represent those who are itinerant evangelists. These men travel from place to place working with, through and for the Church in preaching the good news of Jesus Christ. They do not regularly minister in just one area or with one church or group of churches. Rather, they focus on those communities that invite them for a season of harvest. Some people believe this role is diminishing, but I do not agree. There have been, are, and always will be those called of God to be itinerant evangelists. You may be one of them!

Evangelist-Pastor

Another place of ministry for the evangelist is as an evangelist-pastor. Bill Hybels, John Guest and Steve Jamison are evangelists who serve as pastors of a congregation. Although they are uniquely fashioned to focus most of their ministry in preaching to one church, the Lord uses them beyond that ministry to preach evangelistically in other places.

As mentioned previously, Steve Jamison has been used to minister through Jammin' Against the Darkness, a ministry specifically fashioned to attract those interested in basketball. Steve conducts one or two Jammin' outreach events each year, and through this teen-oriented ministry, he is able to reach thousands of youth with the gospel of Jesus Christ. In addition, Steve receives the support of many church members who work with him in these tremendously successful evangelistic meetings. Evangelist-pastor is certainly a role that fulfills the calling of an evangelist.

Missionary-Evangelist

Some evangelists are missionaries. I use "missionaries" here in a cross-cultural sense. Some missionaries serve as teachers, medical doctors, administrators, and so forth, but many missionaries are also evangelists. Their primary mission is to bring the gospel of Jesus Christ to unreached people groups.

Many of these missionary-evangelists are highly skilled communicators of the gospel who spend years studying a different language and culture in order to powerfully and accurately communicate the gospel of Jesus Christ. They are uniquely formed to love people of different cultures and are motivated by the challenges of new languages, new smells, different living environments, and frequent travel.

Some evangelists who serve cross-culturally often are involved in planting new churches. Doug Venezuela has served in Naples, Italy, for the last 30 years. As a gifted evangelist, he has started several growing and thriving churches. In a dominantly traditional religious culture, the Lord has used Doug's boldness, passion for the lost and great innovative ideas to see hundreds come to Christ and grow in Him.

We commonly refer to such Christian workers as missionaries, not evangelists. However, I think we would be wise to speak of them in a way that God has used them—to win the lost to Christ. Who has the Lord uniquely gifted to fulfill this ministry of harvest? Evangelists! Evangelist-missionary, then, is another ministry path for those seeking to serve the Lord through evangelism.

Church Planter

Many evangelists believe that true evangelism results in planting a new church. In fact, one such church planter recently told me that his definition of an evangelist was "one who preaches the gospel resulting in the lost coming to Christ and a local church being established."

I believe that this is a rather restrictive definition, but one that does have good biblical backing. While I do not think that evangelists are only church planters, I believe that church planting is a vital and viable ministry for those gifted as evangelists. If you feel you are an evangelist and are looking for a way to exercise your calling in the ministry of church planting, you would be wise to seriously consider this avenue of evangelizing.

Church planting allows evangelists to engage their culture with new methods and minimizes traditional structures. Many evangelists love innovation, and church planting allows them to do the "wild and crazy" in some ways. Church planting brings new approaches, new methods, new leaders and new locations to the ministry of evangelism.

Church planting can be highly effective in reaching and winning the lost. Evangelists who successfully build teams around them make tremendous church planters.

Teacher-Evangelist

Some evangelists exhibit powerful teaching gifts. Therefore, I classify some evangelists as teacher-evangelists. These individuals love to equip others in evangelism. Their passion is winning the lost, but they do so primarily through training and mobilizing others.

Many Bible college and seminary professors who teach evangelism fall into this category. They preach well, but their passion for evangelism comes across strongest in the training setting where God uses them to energize their students for the work of evangelism.

Ron Luce, the president of Teen Mania, equips thousands of teenagers each year to effectively share their faith. He is used of God to deliver evangelistic messages and not only sees thousands come to Christ but also mobilizes teens across America to do the same. Dr. Robert Coleman, a teacher and mentor of countless evangelists, also displays this combination of teacher-evangelist. Dr. Coleman has disciplined his life of ministry to teach, train and mentor many students to excel at their ministry of evangelism. He continues to preach on the streets of Boston, mentor students at Gordon Conwell Seminary, and teach seminars and conferences worldwide. As an equipper of the Body of Christ for the work of evangelism, there is no one quite like Dr. Coleman.

Mass evangelism is most effective when hundreds and thousands of believers are mobilized through prayer, personal evangelism and great publicity for the evangelistic event. The Church must be equipped for such large outreaches, and teacher-evangelists can be strategic in this role.

Administrator-Evangelist

Strategies for evangelistic ministry often originate in the hearts and minds of evangelists who have gifts in administration. Crusade directors who serve with mass evangelists (such as Billy Graham, Franklin Graham, Luis Palau and Greg Laurie) exhibit not only.evangelistic passion but also wisdom in focusing the ministry on penetrating a city with the gospel.

Colin James is the vice president of festival ministries for the Luis Palau Evangelistic Association. Colin has a tremendous heart for evangelism, but he also has the gift of wisdom, which manifests itself in the wise decisions he has made in developing evangelistic festivals for Luis Palau. Without a clear understanding of the purpose of the ministry of evangelism, the development of such a mass evangelistic event would get sidetracked. But with a uniquely gifted evangelist who has additional gifts and skills in wisdom, discernment and administration, the Church can be kept on track through the whole process of the evangelistic harvest. Those who share these gifts provide a tremendous service to the Body of Christ in the ministry of evangelism. Additional examples of such individuals are found in the ministries of Luis Bush, the Year 2000 Gospel Movement, and DAWN Ministries.

Writer-Evangelists

For centuries, the written word has also been a powerful means of communicating the good news of Jesus Christ. Authors of many backgrounds, writing styles and creative formats have communicated the powerful story of the good news of Jesus Christ.

Affinity-Group Evangelists

Affinity-group evangelism, such as prison ministry, hospital chaplains and youth ministries, involves focusing on a particular group of people. Some evangelists have a special calling to very specific audiences. Scott Dawson's Pathfinders ministry, Steve Russo's Real Answers for Youth, and Chuck Colson's Prison Fellowship are examples of an affinity-group ministry.

Affinity groups can also be a way of organizing a special season of mass evangelism. Nigel Gordon, the European director for the Luis Palau Association, has been leading affinity-style missions in Eastern European countries for a decade. These missions involve multiple evangelists in multiple cities simultaneously conducting dozens of affinity meetings. These meetings include outreach events to children, youth, professionals, teachers, government officials, taxi drivers and other workers of all kinds. Scott Dawson's book *The Complete Evangelism Guidebook* is an excellent resource for those organizing an evangelistic event for an affinity group.[1]

Apologist-Evangelists

Apologist-evangelists like Josh McDowell and Frank Harber have a passion for giving clear evidence for the validity and verity of the Bible and the gospel. They speak and write on the evidence for a reasonable faith. Apologist-evangelists have a deep concern for intellectual integrity, passion for the truth, and sincere concern for those without Christ to hear and understand the evidence for a reasonable faith. Although they debate atheists, agnostics and evolutionists on university campuses and elsewhere, their primary concern is that people encounter the resurrected Jesus Christ.

In addition to their passion for giving clear evidence for a reasonable faith, these evangelists have a passion for the lost. This is expressed in their boldness to engage those who are often anti-Christian and seek to openly confront their particular view of truth and evidence for a reasonable faith. Although some scholars emphasize that the purpose of apologetics is for strengthening the faith of those who already believe, presentations of the foundations for believing do nonetheless have a powerful impact on those who do not yet believe.

Just recently, George Hogdon, a lay evangelist from Tillamook, Oregon, shared his journey to faith with me, which included a presentation of the gospel from an apologetic point of view. During his college years, he began his own exploration for truth and ultimate reality, but only in Christ and through the witness of many followers of Jesus did he actually come to decide for himself that Jesus is the way, the truth and the life. So apologist-evangelists definitely play a key role in the salvation journey of many followers of Jesus Christ.

Probably one of the best known and most loved apologist-evangelists is Francis Schaeffer. Although Schaeffer was initially a missionary to children in Switzerland, his compassionate heart and keen mind played a huge role in clarifying the gospel for a generation of lost Baby Boomers in the mid-1960s through the early 1980s. Schaeffer gave reasonable answers to the dilemma facing the Church in its witness to the world, studied the social issues of his day, and explained the bankruptcy of living autonomously from God.

Society said that God did not exist, but Schaeffer pointed out that though it may seem God is silent, in fact He is not. God speaks constantly through His Word, His people and the events of history. The question actually is, Are we listening? And the questions for the Church are, Are we filled with compassion? Are we listening to the cries of the lost? Does our compassion lead us to think deeply about the way in which we communicate the gospel?

Schaeffer created a specific vocabulary to clarify his explanation of the gospel. Although he was primarily an apologist who gave reasoned answers to the questions confronting the Church, he did capture the minds and hearts of many questioning Christians concerning the intelligence of their faith.

Television and Radio Evangelists

For decades, television and radio have been effective avenues for Christians to preach the gospel of Jesus Christ and influence the culture in powerful ways. In fact, Luis Palau says that if he had only one means of preaching the gospel, he would use radio—a powerful statement that should awaken some to the tremendous opportunity radio and television evangelism afford. However, because of the number of people who can be influenced through the airwaves, those whom God has called to use these awesome means to communicate the good news of Jesus Christ carry an extra responsibility for each word they say.

Internet Evangelists

The last decade has seen the explosion of new technology, such as the Internet. One of our Next Generation Alliance evangelists, Rusty Wright, uses the Internet as an effective twenty-first century means of evangelism. Rusty writes:

> "He tried for 40 years!" said the subject line in my e-mail inbox. Was it junk e-mail or Internet spam? I even contemplated deleting it. Here, slightly edited (and with emphasis added), is what the e-mail said:
>
>> *Can you help?* I am 65, was born in Greece, came to America when I was 17, and spent at least 25 years in almost 35 different churches to convince myself that there is a God. Have truly kept an open mind but cannot in all honesty accept such an intangible faith.
>>
>> Have been married for 42 years to a great lady, very much a believer. Have gone to her church many times, *but always leave empty-hearted.* My parents and two sisters have been strong believers ever since I can remember. I have been a very strong believer in honesty, fairness, loyalty and compassion. *I feel almost cheated with my honest inability to believe in God.* Can you help me?

This dear seeker apparently had read one of my articles at www.probe.org. My reply complimented him for his dedicated search for God and commitment to honorable living. Millions use the web daily, many seeking spiritual answers. Perhaps you could use this as a ministry for evangelism as I do.[2]

Although there are many ministries expressing Christ's compassion for the lost, at the center there is always a gifted person speaking and leading the people of God into greater service for Christ. In John 14:12, Jesus spoke of the greater works the disciples would do. I believe evangelists lead the Church in the great works of evangelization. The Lord calls and gifts evangelists to lead the Church in dynamic and effective evangelism, and we need to keep our minds and hearts open wide to the variety of unique giftedness these evangelists bring in. I trust that this chapter has challenged your thinking on how God uses evangelists to embolden and mobilize the Church for effective harvest—and how Christ can use you, too!

Notes

1. Scott Dawson, *The Complete Evangelism Guidebook* (Grand Rapids, MI: Baker Book House, 2006).
2. Rusty Wright, Probe Ministries, P.O. Box 702, Mount Hermon, California, 95041-0702, e-mail message to author, May 2002.

CHAPTER 7

NOTHING IS MORE IMPORTANT

THE PRIORITY OF EVANGELISTIC MINISTRY

LUIS PALAU

Then Jesus came to them and said, "All authority in heaven and on earth has been given to me. Therefore go and make disciples of all nations, baptizing them in the name of the Father and of the Son and of the Holy Spirit, and teaching them to obey everything I have commanded you. And surely I am with you always, to the very end of the age."

MATTHEW 28:18-20

A while back, the missions committee of a supporting church wrote to let us know that they were cutting support of our evangelistic association by 50 percent. Paraphrased, the letter said, "We love you. We think the world of you. But giving is down. May God provide for your needs." Nothing unusual—I'm sure every missions organization gets letters like this.

In the same envelope, however, was the church's weekly bulletin. One announcement caught my attention: "The pastor and twenty men in the church will be leaving this week with their wives for a golf tournament in the Bahamas. Pray for them."

Now, I'm all for golf tournaments. Golf is a fine game. And these 21 couples can spend their money any way they want. But I confess it bothered me to know that in this church, hitting and chasing a little white ball seemed to be a greater priority than evangelistic ministry.

"The work of conversion is the first and great thing we must drive at; after this we must labour with all our might," said Charles H. Spurgeon, the great nineteenth-century British preacher. And John Wesley reminded preachers, "You have nothing to do but to save souls."

I believe evangelism is the main work of the Church of Jesus Christ. I've debated that point with many good friends, including one of my mentors, who believed that if you build up the local church and worship right on Sunday morning, emphasizing solid biblical exposition, the people will automatically give witness to their faith at work and around the community come Monday.

At the World Congress on Evangelism in Berlin in 1966, one of evangelical Christianity's most respected statesmen said, "Evangelism happens when the people of God walk with God." But 30 years of experience tells me that it doesn't work that way. I know great worshiping people who just don't share their faith, and godly men and women for whom evangelism never happens. If evangelism happened naturally, the Lord wouldn't have repeatedly commanded it. Evangelism must stay a priority for us to continue the work of Christ.

THE CHURCH'S (FORGOTTEN) NUMBER ONE PRIORITY

Evangelism is a chosen act of obedience to God's revealed will. It is the highest, most important act of obedience for a Christian, because there is nothing more important to God, "who wants all men to be saved" (1 Tim. 2:4). "The Lord . . . is patient with you, not wanting anyone to perish, but everyone to come to repentance" (2 Pet. 3:9).

Jesus made His mission very plain: "For the Son of Man came to seek and to save what was lost" (Luke 19:10). We know His final command to "go and make disciples of all nations" (Matt. 28:19) as the Great Commission, not the Great *Suggestion*.

Unfortunately, it's a commission largely ignored today.[1] There are pockets of action, thank God, but evangelism isn't a priority—let alone *the* priority—for thousands of churches and Christians in America. Since 1990, when our association began to focus much of our ministry on helping to re-evangelize America, my team and I have led evangelistic festivals in more than a dozen cities in the United States. In each one, evangelism has been warfare, and too many of its most vehement opponents have been Christians. It takes an excruciating effort to persuade many Christians just to come to an evangelistic meeting, let alone to pray for unsaved friends, practice friendship evangelism, and invite friends to come along to hear the gospel in a quality setting.

I understand that the method—festival evangelism—is sometimes the focus of some churches' misguided opposition, not evangelism itself. But our team members, through months of preparation, prayer and training for a festival in a city, and visits to scores of churches to get to know their pastors, have discovered that most churches devote very little time to evangelism of *any* kind.

Sometimes opposition to a particular method of evangelism cloaks defensiveness about the content of the gospel itself. Some church members, embarrassed about the gospel, would rather keep the light under a bushel.

In reality, arguing against a method is almost always a smoke screen for inaction. As D. L. Moody told one critic who didn't approve of his mass evangelism methods, "I don't like them too much myself. What methods do *you* use?" When the critic indicated he didn't use any evangelistic tools or activities, Moody said, "Well, I like the way I do it better than the way you don't."

PLEASE EXCUSE ME

Still, critics and nonparticipants abound. Here's a list of the most common excuses we hear for not getting involved in a citywide evangelistic festival:

- "We have our own evangelistic programs." *Fine. Let's work together and extend the Kingdom!*

- "We are too busy." *But are you about the Lord's most important work?*

- "The deacons won't let our church get involved." *Why not? Let's talk and pray about it.*

- "We don't believe in evangelism." *What exactly do you believe? Is your church a Christian church?*

- "We don't believe in your form of evangelism." *Festival evangelism encompasses a wide variety of methods. Which do you prefer?*

- "We don't want to make a show of evangelism." *Agreed. Let's work together to exalt Jesus Christ, not the event or the evangelists.*

- "People who make a decision to follow Christ at festivals never continue in their relationship with the Lord." *Actually, research of several of our festivals has shown that more than 70 percent of those who make a decision to follow Christ are active members of a local church six months after the festivals.*[2]

- "You are not contemporary enough." *I suppose it depends on which festival event you attend.*

- "You are too contemporary." *Please stay home on youth night.*

- "Festivals don't work anymore." *George Barna, Russell Chandler, C. Peter Wagner and others have said that perhaps the greatest festivals in American history are yet ahead.*

- "Our church is already full—we don't have room for any more." *Great! Let's work together and help fill other churches.*

- "Right now our church is into prayer ministry." *Are you praying by name each day for your unsaved neighbors, relatives and friends? Let's tell them the gospel together.*

- "We have to build up our saints first before we can do evangelism." *What better way to disciple them than by getting them actively involved in helping fulfill the Great Commission? According to the apostle Paul, God uses the gospel and the proclamation of Jesus Christ to "establish" believers (see Rom. 16:25).*

- "We are in the middle of a building project." *Great! Let's work together to build God's kingdom at the same time and fill up your church with new believers in Christ.*

George Barna issues a wake-up call to Christians to "get into the game and share the good news, now!"[3] He adds, "How ironic that during this period of swelling need for the proclamation of the gospel and the healing powers of the church, the ranks of the messengers have dissipated to anemic proportions."[4]

STIMULATE TO WITNESS

The Luis Palau Evangelistic Association's mission is not only to win as many people as possible to Jesus Christ but also to stimulate, train and mobilize the Church to continuous, effective evangelism and follow-up and growth. A festival helps to renew churches so that they can be more effective in their evangelistic ministries. If they don't have an evangelism program, we want to help them get one going. If they have one that's not working well, we want to help infuse it with power. And if they have a dynamic program, we hope to give it a boost of energy and join with them in teaching others how to win people to Christ.

Maranatha Bible Church in Grand Rapids, Michigan, where our team held a festival recently, serves as an example of what can happen. The pastor, John Campbell, enthusiastically brought the festival opportunity before his board. It elicited much debate, which centered on the many denominations involved. The final vote was six in favor, five opposed.

Although disheartened that the vote was so close, the pastor challenged all of the elders and deacons to get involved in some aspect of the festival—and they did. After the event, there was unanimous agreement that the festival was an overwhelming blessing for everyone in the congregation. Each board member who was previously opposed to the church's involvement had become a festival supporter.

One elder praised the training. Another was impressed with the spirit of oneness and cooperation among people from different denominations. One man said that his attitude changed during the friendship evangelism training, particularly when another man in the church stood up and reported that after the first session, he was burdened to pray and share the gospel with a seriously ill coworker. Two days later, he led his coworker to Christ.

"God has changed our hearts," Pastor Campbell said. "Our church board and our congregation have more compassion for the lost than they ever had before. God used our involvement in the crusade as a springboard to move our church's focus from an inward one to an outward one. They saw God working in and through this festival to bring people to salvation in His Son, and it has changed us permanently. Thank God."

SINGLE-MINDED RESCUERS

On June 2, 1995, Captain Scott O'Grady, an Air Force F-16 pilot, was shot down by a surface-to-air missile just south of the Bosnian city of Banja Luka. He evaded capture for more than six days before finally being rescued by a Marine Corps search and rescue team.

After his dramatic rescue, my friend Jim Reapsome compared the mission of the Church to the Marines' heroism. Jim bemoaned many churches' wasted energy in battles over peripheral matters, such as praise choruses versus traditional hymns.

"The devil is having a field day, because every such intramural fight is a gain for his schemes to keep us from doing our primary mission—

breaking down the walls of his kingdom of darkness and rescuing people for God's kingdom of light," Jim wrote. "[The Marines who rescued Captain O'Grady] did not sit around and argue about which arrangement of the Marine Corps hymn to sing. They pursued a single mission—rescue a downed pilot—and they allowed nothing to sidetrack them."

Jim concluded, "As the old saying goes, we must keep the main thing the main thing, which is to throw lifelines of hope and peace to people trampled and overcome by despair."[5]

In today's Church, there simply isn't a conviction to get out the simple, unadorned gospel of John 3:16-18 and 1 Corinthians 15:1-3. I easily get emotional when I think about that gospel message, which comes directly from the heart of God. Every time we preach, we must let people know that God loves them. He is actively looking for them.

Thanks to the missionaries who brought that message to South America, both my father and mother are in heaven. Shortly before my father died of a sudden, severe illness when he was only 34 years old, he sat up in bed and, struggling to breathe, began to sing, "Bright crowns up there, bright crowns for you and me." Then he fell back on his pillow and said, "I'm going to be with Jesus, which is far better." A few years ago, my mother joined him in heaven. Thank God for the gospel message and for the missionaries who sacrificially brought it to us with its assurance of eternal life (see John 10:28)!

DESPERATE TO PERSUADE

In today's Church, part of the reason why there's no urgency to evangelize is because we don't deeply believe that the lost are really lost. We don't out and out deny it, because that would sound heretical; but we don't embrace it, because if we did, we'd be much more *desperate* to persuade lost and dying people to turn to Christ.

"Each man's life is but a breath" (Ps. 39:5), and then we enter eternity—either eternal joy with God in heaven or eternal torment in hell. "God keeps no halfway house," evangelist Billy Sunday preached. "It's either heaven or hell for you and me."

"The moment a soul drops the body, and stands naked before God, it cannot but know what its portion will be to all eternity," John Wesley said. "It will have full in its view, either everlasting joy or everlasting torment."

I have a friend whose mother is dying without Christ, yet he doesn't seem to feel the same despair that I feel—and she's not my mother. I know my friend cares, but if my mother were dying without Christ, I think I'd spend every day on my knees by her bed until she surrendered to the Savior.

One of my team members, David, received word at our Portland office that his father-in-law, Mr. Stevens, had only hours to live in a Minnesota hospital halfway across the country. For years, Mr. Stevens had refused to listen to his daughter Gayle and David's appeals to give his life to Christ. He was mad at God because his wife had died 40 years earlier of cancer.

David rushed home, phoned the hospital room, and asked a nurse to hold the phone to his father-in-law's ear. "Dad, you've got only a few hours to live," he said. "Soon you're going to face your Creator. Isn't it time to get things right with the Lord?" Despite having tubes in his mouth and nose, the old fellow managed to say, "Yes." David quickly went through the Four Spiritual Laws, and then asked, "Would you like to receive Christ?" Mr. Stevens prayed aloud with David, confessing his sins and committing to trust in Jesus Christ. Overjoyed that her dad would be with the Lord, Gayle promised her husband, "You don't ever have to buy me another gift, for no gift can match knowing I'll see Daddy again in heaven."

In his book *Evangelism That Works*, George Barna tells about Bill Hybels's sermon on the rich man and Lazarus. Barna says that chills ran down his spine as Pastor Hybels passionately read the plaintive cry of the rich man, who was in torment in hell, to Abraham: "I beg you, father, send Lazarus to my father's house, for

I have five brothers. Let him warn them, so that they will not also come to this place of torment" (Luke 16:27-28).

Barna states, "To this day, more than a decade later, I recall that lesson and the horror that filled me as I realized, perhaps for the first time, how horrific a life in hell would be, how significant the death of Christ had been for me, and just how imperative it is to use every resource available to share the real truth about life, death, sin, and grace with every person I know."[6]

Barna could not sleep that night, knowing that many of his friends and family members would join Lazarus in eternal torment unless somebody told them the gospel of Jesus Christ. He knew the "somebody" was meant to be him. His life as an evangelizer hasn't been the same since.

All of us could use a few restless nights. Let's pray for restless nights, for burning tears, for sobs of compassion.

After all, the number one responsibility of a Christian is not to retire young in order to spend endless hours chasing a little white golf ball. If only people could get as excited about building the kingdom of God as they do about their handicap on the golf course.

Yes, evangelism is spiritual warfare. In evangelism, we engage Satan nose to nose and try to steal his prey. So we should expect a few doors slammed in our face and more severe attacks on ourselves and our families.

But there's near ecstatic joy in obeying the Lord. A few inconveniences such as cynicism, rejection and, yes, even imprisonment only seemed to heighten the happiness of Jesus' first-century followers.

"As soon as ever you have won a soul, you won't care about any of the other things," Moody said. There's no greater thrill than giving out the gospel and leading people into the eternal kingdom of God Almighty. So give evangelism all you've got. This life is your only chance.

Notes

1. George Barna, *Evangelism That Works: How to Reach Changing Generations with the Unchanging Gospel* (Ventura, CA: Regal Books, 1995), pp. 35-36. According to a 1994 survey by the Barna Research Group, 9 out of 10 adults cannot even define the meaning of the Great Commission. "It is one of the defining commands of Jesus, given as a core challenge to all of His followers, and a central element in the stated mission of churches, denominations, and parachurch organizations worldwide. But the typical American adult, who has undoubtedly been exposed to this long-standing challenge many times, has no recollection of the content of the challenge."

2. Three of the most in-depth follow-up studies were conducted by Roy Pointer with Bible Society, Peter Brierley with MARC Europe (two separate studies of Mission to London, 1983-1984), and Henry J. Schmidt (Central California Crusade, 1986-1987).

3. Barna, *Evangelism That Works,* p. 15.

4. Ibid., p. 22.

5. Jim Reapsome, "Capt. O'Grady's Life Line," *Pulse* (July 21, 1995), p. 8.

6. Barna, *Evangelism That Works,* pp. 12-13.

CHAPTER 8

FIRST THINGS FIRST

PURSUING EVANGELISTIC MINISTRY

TIMOTHY ROBNETT

Some evangelists' calling will not involve launching a brand-new ministry. Many will fill previously established positions in church or denominational administrations, parachurch ministries, and the like. Other evangelists will, however, feel the entrepreneurial bug bite and build new ministry teams.

No matter what our workplace, we all must begin by asking ourselves some basic questions, the most important one being, *What has God called me uniquely to do in service for Him?*

CALLING

In 1 Samuel 3, the young boy Samuel had to learn to recognize and understand the voice of God. Certainly, the applications of the text could be many, but the lesson of learning to hear the voice of God and respond to Him speaks to the issue of clarifying our call to evangelistic ministry.

The first and second time the Lord spoke to Samuel, the boy ran to the priest Eli and said, "Here I am; you called me" (vv. 5,6). But when the Lord spoke the third time to Samuel, we hear the response that God longs for: "Speak, for your servant is listening" (v. 10). As evangelists, we need to clarify in our own hearts the fact that God is calling us to a specific ministry.

Isaiah also was confronted by God's need for workers in the harvest. Isaiah 6:8 says, "Then I heard the voice of the Lord saying, 'Whom shall I send? And who will go for us?' And I said, 'Here am I. Send me!'" Untold numbers of believers in Jesus Christ have responded to this call throughout the centuries.

On a Sunday late in the winter months of 1970, I was just a few weeks away from leaving home for Stanford University. Our youth pastor, Will Moir, was preaching from Isaiah 6 that Sunday morning. Possibly I had heard the message before, but never so personally. That morning, the Lord touched my heart in a very moving way. He touched not so much my emotions as my will—not to bring tears to my eyes but to bend my will with the desire to follow Him no matter the direction or cost. A number of us responded to an invitation to come to the altar that day, and as I stood among friends, young and old, the Lord's voice seemed so personal, so real, as if He stood among us.

Today, decades later, I still remember that moment. For me, this memorial moment continues to assure me that the call was for me, for a lifetime. How about you? When did you receive the message for ministry? Where were you? Who else was there? To remember is to refresh your soul and keep your direction focused on the goal.

In 1 Timothy 1:18-19, Paul reminded Timothy that God's call to him was confirmed by the church, and that though God had spoken to him personally, others were witnesses of the gifting and calling upon his life. How has God confirmed your calling as an evangelist? Who confirmed it? When? These affirmations will give you confidence, not in yourself, but in God's working through your life. Jesus said we would know the kind of tree it is by the fruit it bears. Even so, the fruit of abiding in Christ stems from His working in us (see John 15:1-16).

Sometimes, Timothy lost his boldness and energy for ministry. Paul wrote to encourage and motivate him to keep doing God's work. Evangelist, you may be discouraged—this is to be expected from our earthly journey—but don't discount God's calling and ministry in your life. Timothy didn't, and neither should you.

As a pastor, Timothy was also called to "do the work of telling the Good News" (2 Tim. 4:5, NCV). In some translations, such as the New International Version, this verse reads, "Do the work of an evangelist." Many questions come to mind when reading this verse: Who is an evangelist? How many evangelists are there in the Body of Christ? Are all evangelists men? Are all evangelists those who preach to the masses?

It is difficult to answer many of these questions. Certainly, we need to ask, "What is the outcome of a lifetime of ministry?" The fruit demonstrates the root. If your life is motivated by winning the lost and seeing fruit in regard to that work, I would say that you are an evangelist. If there is a lot of talk but no fruit, then the question is not only gifting and calling but also maturity in Christ.

If you are an evangelist who desires to form your own ministry, the essential first step is to clarify your calling to this ministry. There are many rewards of establishing your own ministry under the leadership of the Holy Spirit, but there are also many pressures and obstacles. But the core of the issue is in your own heart. What is God asking you to do?

VISION

Evangelists need to crystallize their call into a personal vision statement. Luis Palau consistently desires to preach to as many people as possible. No matter what other strengths and abilities Luis has, at the end of the day his plans include some type of large meeting: crusade, festival, rally, and so forth. Why? Because this is Luis's unique vision. The more the better! Not everyone is called to or gifted for this type of ministry, but for Luis, this is God's plan.

What is your unique vision? Who is God calling you to reach? Where do they live? Is it the youth of America? Is it the youth of the world? Is it the 65 million elderly of China today who are undernourished and lack shelter and clothing? Will you go? What's your vision—that personal call of God for you in your lifetime—to make a difference? When all is said and done, what is it that you want to have done? Will you be satisfied? Will you be able to say to the Father as Jesus said, "I have brought you glory on earth by completing the work you gave me to do" (John 17:4)?

OBEDIENCE

Another major issue is obedience. Jesus calls us to a life of obedience, to follow Him no matter the assignment, the cost, the place or the time.

Evangelists need to be obedient to the One who has called them (see Matt. 10; Luke 9). It is far easier to say "God has called me to preach the good news" than to actually go and do it. God needs obedient evangelists. There is a cost of conveniences lost, family left behind and material rewards given up, yet Christ is asking us to go. Many evangelists travel from place to place. Some focus on a local church or area. But all have a story to tell to the towns, cities and nations.

Philip, the noted evangelist in the New Testament, began his ministry by traveling. The Scriptures indicate that he left Jerusalem for Samaria and then made his way to several coastal cities, the road to Egypt, and then to Caesarea, where he seems to have settled down (see Acts 8:26-40). Are you ready to travel?

This is an important issue for a number of reasons. A life of indulgence has ruined more than one evangelist in our time. Are you mature in the Lord and able to resist the temptations that come with travel? Are you disciplined and able to be productive when you travel? Are you humble and able to serve others while you travel? Are you a good steward of time and money as you travel? Can you maintain healthy family relationships at home while you're away? Is your spouse totally supportive of your ministry, even when it requires you to be absent from home for extended periods of time? The itinerant-evangelist's lifestyle is unique, and not all people are suited for it. Are you? This is part of obedience to the call, but it's also an issue that can assist you in clarifying the call. If you don't travel well, possibly the Lord has another assignment for you.

Obedience can require radical changes in ministry style. In Acts 16, we read about what is known as the Macedonian Call. Paul and his team, though seasoned in ministry, were confronted with a different assignment from the Lord. First, the Lord stopped their progress in Asia, then spoke clearly to them about a greater need, and finally confirmed the call to go to Europe. Obedience sometimes requires radical and speedy change. Are you open to new assignments? The Spirit of Christ often redirects us. Are you flexible? Are you available? Are you connected with the voice of Christ?

Martha Wagner, one of the NGA evangelists, received a challenge from the Lord at the Proclamation Evangelism Network conference in Fort Lauderdale, Florida, in March 2003. The Spirit of the Lord gave her a vision to create a multimedia presentation of the good news for the women of America. The Spirit of Jesus was asking Martha to develop a new approach to ministry that would require obedience, creativity, and trust in the Lord. Martha obeyed, and her newly created presentation, "Better Than a Story," has been viewed by thousands of women, with hundreds coming into a new relationship with Jesus Christ. Jesus asks us to obey, and He promises to be with us in these new ventures. Are you obeying what the Lord has asked you to do?

TEAMWORK

Jesus has not called us to serve Him as Lone Rangers. Jesus, by the working of His Spirit, calls us to work in teams. Coach Lopez, my son Joel's track coach at West View High in Beaverton, Oregon, challenged his team members with the idea that team is better than solo. This is an interesting statement from a track coach, yet his words remind us of what we already know: When it comes to advancing the good news of Jesus, together the Church can do far more than one lone Christian. Some evangelists tend to go it alone. *It's hard enough to get along with yourself, much less others,* they think. Yet, when evangelists submit to the Spirit and learn to lead a team, greater works will be done.

The Bible teaches that teams are part of Christ's strategy for evangelizing the world. He chose 12 men to train and send out to do evangelism. The apostles worked in teams. Paul developed teams around him throughout his lifetime. Teams are described by the Holy Spirit in gifting the Church with apostles, prophets, evangelists, pastors and teachers. The pictures of the Church as a body and a building imply multiplicity of gifting and ministry. We need each other—God designed it that way.

Why does the evangelist need a team? Because while evangelists have great gifts, they also have glaring weaknesses. Many evangelists have great abilities to inspire but are weak in following through on the details. Many evangelists can challenge and create vision but are awkward at developing plans and processes. Many evangelists may normally be high emotionally, but sometimes in the low moments they may become destructive to themselves and others. Evangelists need teams around them to bring balance, wisdom and focus. Obviously, when one tries to do it all, a lot doesn't get done.

As I have observed the Luis Palau Association, I have discovered a number of unique teams. The Latin team, which has been headed by Dr. Jim Williams and Ruben Peretti for almost 30 years, was the original team the Lord brought to work with Luis Palau in South America, and it has grown in number and impact. After years of service together, they have conducted hundreds of crusades and festivals in the Spanish-speaking world. They have developed a unique style of work and play, and at the core of their relationship, they have a high regard for one another and a clear vision for their work together. Some of the greatest festivals for the Latin team have come in just the last few years—800,000 in Buenos Aires, Argentina; 650,000 in Lima, Peru; and 85,000 in Madrid, Spain.

Three individuals in the Luis Palau Association stand out as team participants. As mentioned above, Jim Williams has served with Luis for more than 30 years. Jim brings a reflective and biblical approach to things. He thinks deeply and seeks to assure the team that the Lord has been consulted in all things.

David Jones came to the team in the late 1970s. As a journalist, he was recruited to handle all media, but David's gifts of administration and management naturally led to his role as the vice president of administration. He handles many matters and keeps them all in logical order. His love for media continues to assist the team in strategic media projects, but he also excels in managing the affairs of the whole team.

Doug Steward is a man for all seasons as a worker and a saint. Doug has overseen the Association's radio, television and video productions for years, confident that the Lord is with us. He has recorded untold numbers of Luis's messages. He has designed and operated stage productions for Luis Palau crusades and festivals. He has made the meetings happen from various angles. Doug has been a servant at all times with more than his share of godly wisdom to solve what seemed to be unsolvable problems. From 1979 to 1990, Luis's team was centered around these three faithful men. Without them, there would not have been a foundation for the years of growth that have followed.

The latest development in the team concept for Luis has come with the maturing of his three sons. Kevin, Keith and Andrew have now spent from 10 to 20 years involved in growing the ministry. They have learned well from their dad. They are each unique, yet they flourish in their team roles in leadership, development and communicating the good news. The future is bright because "T.E.A.M." still reflects how ministry is done at the Luis Palau Evangelistic Association.

Do you have a team? Who is on your team? If you are just starting out, who should be your first team member? Possibly you're a gifted believer who loves evangelism, but like many in the Luis Palau Association, you may have other gifts that are crucial to the success of an evangelist and his or her ministry.

BUILDING A MINISTRY

Where does a godly team come from? First, you need a clear vision. Second, you need to pray. The Bible says we are to "ask the Lord of the harvest" for laborers in the harvest (Matt. 9:38). Then begin talking with others in ministry who know you and understand your vision. Networking with other evangelists, pastors and missionaries will greatly assist you in seeking the right team members. Also, ask yourself, *Who have I served with? Who have I observed in ministry?*

As you think seriously about the people to serve with you, you need to be sure:

- They share your vision.
- They are committed to the Lord, no matter the cost.
- They love evangelism.
- They are committed for the long term—for years, not just months.
- They are honest people—with themselves, you and God.
- They are team players.

Even evangelists whom God has called to develop their own ministry outside a specific church or denomination do not serve the Lord autonomously. There is one Lord of the Church and one Church. Although the Church has many local expressions, as God has designed, an evangelist still needs to function under the authority of a local church or denomination. How does this happen?

An evangelist can serve under the authority and structure of a denomination. The Assembly of God, Southern Baptist and Nazarene churches all have positions for ordained evangelists. If evangelists are not serving with or under a denominational structure, they need to obtain the full support and endorsement of their local church.

When the evangelistic ministry is formed, it must be registered with the government. This formal registration requires that the association have bylaws, articles of incorporation and a board of directors. These documents of incorporation and the individuals chosen to serve the association should reflect biblical principles for operation. (For more information on this process, please contact the Luis Palau Association Next Generation Alliance using the contact information at the back of this book.)

To stay true to God and the work of His Church, it is essential that you be accountable through public and private reports. In Acts 14–15, the apostles gave reports to the Jerusalem Council on the progress and problems of their ministry. Similarly, evangelists need to give honest and clear reports to their board, church, denomination and constituency concerning what the Lord has given them to do and what the results are. In addition, all financial recording and reporting should be in compliance with normal business practices.

Evangelistic ministries, as with local churches and missions organizations, have seasons of ministry. Growth and development are the result of faith and hard work. Ministries will grow as leadership grows. Evangelists have precious gifts and are needed by the Church to do the work of harvesting. They need to sharpen their gifts and become better at what God has given them to do. How do they do this? First, they stay in fellowship with other evangelists. Second, they study the culture in which they serve the Lord. Third, they take advanced studies at seminaries or universities, and they attend seminars and conferences. Evangelists need to be learners.

Organizational growth and expansion come as the evangelist learns to be a leader of a ministry, not just a communicator of the good news. Many evangelists spend a lifetime without a team, and the Lord uses them in many wonderful ways. You may be such an evangelist. God bless you! However, if you want to grow your ministry and lead an organization successfully, you will need to learn skills in leadership and management. (Again, Next Generation Alliance will be glad to assist you in understanding this process and come alongside of you to coach you as you grow.)

Jose Zayas reflects the values of the Next Generation Alliance. Beyond being its first director, Jose was one of the first evangelists launched by the NGA. He grew through observing Dr. Palau during his seven years on staff, asked counsel and support for launching Jose Zayas Evangelism International, received support staff and a facility to assist in birthing his new ministry, and maintained relationships with many of the LPEA staff. Jose is a tremendous communicator of the good news, but even more, he is a faith-filled evangelist who, in his own humble way, continues to seek counsel and assistance to grow his ministry for the Lord.

Steve Wingfield has also accelerated the growth of his ministry through Next Generation Alliance. In 1997, Steve already had a well-established ministry, but he found that NGA was extremely helpful in training his staff. From the training of festival directors and development personnel to understanding Steve's role as an evangelist and leader, NGA helped Steve's ministry to more than double its capacity in five years.

Leadership and management can be learned. Evangelists who want to extend the impact of their ministry far beyond their current levels need to grow as leaders and managers. When they do, they will experience a greater degree of God's provision for their vision.

Practicing Faith

The Church needs men and women of faith to stretch the vision of reaching our generation with the good news of Jesus Christ. Evangelists have a great measure of faith and are typically the ones God uses to challenge the Church to great works. Often, the Church seems more concerned about preservation than proclamation. Both are essential, but it is evangelists who typically champion the proclamation side of the issue.

The Word of God is clear that "without faith it is impossible to please God" (Heb. 11:6). Faith is often simplified into mere belief; however, "faith" is a word with many dimensions. Obviously, belief in the knowledge of God is essential for faith. But faith also requires trusting God to act when we cannot, which requires not only our intellectual assent but also the expectation that God will intervene in our lives and the lives of others. Faith also requires discernment and a hunger for righteousness.

Evangelist, you are needed by the Church today. Your great

dreams and visions are needed to keep the Church on the cutting edge of culture and history. Although you may be misunderstood and your ministry may be marginalized, God is calling you to greater faith and works for Him. He is asking that you don't leave those in the Church behind but that you invite them to be that irresistible Church of love and truth in a dark and depressed world.

So, evangelist, where's that gigantic, humanly impossible yet God-focused dream? The world is waiting for you to work with, through and for the Church to answer the Lord's question, "Who will go for Me?" Will you say, as you have said before, "Lord, here I am. Send me!"?

CHAPTER 9

Now What?

Building an Evangelistic Ministry

Luis Palau

When I was a young man living in Argentina, I wanted to go into full-time evangelism. Unfortunately, there were several obstacles in my way.

First, our denomination didn't have evangelists. Second, my job at the bank provided the main source of income for myself, my mother and my little sisters. And then there was the fact that I didn't know how to evangelize.

But there was also what I had read about in many magazines—the "call."

People like to say, "I'm waiting for the call" or "I don't know if I have the call." I once read a little pamphlet by a great missionary in China entitled "I Was Never Called."

My mother was the one who kept pushing me to go into evangelism. Even though I had a good job at the bank and was the only source of income for our family, she kept encouraging me to go into evangelism and church planting. She was persistent, never raising her voice, but continually pushing me to pursue it.

One day I replied to her, "I'm waiting for the call."

I've never forgotten her response. "The call, the call," she said. "The call went out 2,000 years ago. The Lord is waiting for the response, not the call!"

Evangelism is a matter of obedience. Every Christian is called to witness. But some of us have the gift of evangelism. The main difference is that evangelists have a special push to win souls—a special desire to do something more than just witnessing during the course of everyday life.

People with a gift of evangelism have that extra push. They are not more holy or spiritual or devoted than the rest of the people who witness as they work every day, but the Holy Spirit pushes them to want to do more. This is a good indicator that you have the gift of evangelism—you have a hunger to see people come into the kingdom of God.

Another indicator is that when you preach, people get excited about the gospel. Or if someone you trust comes up and says, "You really have the gift of evangelism."

BE HOLY

Let's say you know you have the call. You have the gift. You feel a deep desire for evangelism. Now what?

Having a successful evangelistic ministry begins with our personal lives as evangelists. First, we must have a transparent conscience—no unresolved conflicts or skeletons in the closets. We confess our sin every day.

Second, truthfulness must mark our words and our writing. When I report on the results from a festival, I must honor God with the truth. "Evangelistically speaking" is a byword in many countries. It indicates evangelists' tendency to exaggerate. What an embarrassing indictment!

Third, the glory of God should be the deepest longing of our inner spirits. How ugly to think that when engaging in the most sacred task of preaching God's good news, we would mingle a desire for personal fame with it. No wonder the Lord Jesus had to bear so much on that cross to cleanse such shameful self-seeking. We must train ourselves in the Spirit's power to incessantly give God all the glory and all the praise. He alone—our Creator—is worthy.

Proverbs 22:1 says, "A good name is more desirable than great riches; to be esteemed is better than silver or gold." Reputation is first. We work for it, of course, like everyone else in the world. However, as evangelists, we must work especially hard to maintain it, or we soon lose out. And we must have reputable men of God to oversee our finances so that the enemy cannot blaspheme Jesus Christ. We are to do all things honestly so that we "make the teaching about God our Savior attractive" (Titus 2:10).

Watch out for things that can tear your reputation apart. Evangelists who make commitments but don't keep them, who convince themselves that they are superior to others, or who threaten those who won't go along with their pet projects permanently tarnish their reputations.

Another downfall can come from competing with other evangelists. If you find yourself envying someone who seems more successful than you, write down two or three major things that are excellent or positive about the person you envy. Ask God to help you focus on His work, not your own.

An evil, destructive, critical, petty spirit has caused the downfall of scores of people I know in evangelism. Hebrews 12:15 says, "See to it that no one misses the grace of God and that no bitter root grows up to cause trouble." That bitter root can destroy you. Watch for it. Confess it. Crucify it!

Another downfall for us as evangelists can result from trying to keep down any up-and-coming younger evangelists who are seeing results, thinking they might overtake us, pass us up and outshine us. It is embarrassing to even confess that such thoughts cross our minds—but they do.

Holiness says, "We are in this together to the glory of Jesus Christ. We are fellow servants, fellow evangelists." Hard on the ego, but glorifying to Jesus! Only God the Holy Spirit can work that in me. He is eager. Are we?

Seek Advice

Every evangelist ought to be accountable to the elders of his or her own local family church. Even though an evangelist may be well known and loved, it does not follow that he or she is independent from God's rules of life. The local church is God's provision for joy, holiness, growth, maturing and, when necessary, church discipline.

Remember that God has provided godly, mature Christian men as counselors. "In abundance of counselors there is victory," we read in Proverbs 11:14 (*NASB*). Mature brothers and sisters are our protection. Over and over again, Proverbs tells us that the wise man receives reproof, but the fool scoffs. How many "fools" I have seen fall all the way to the bottom.

One day at a youth congress in Germany, Billy Graham told me that most evangelists quit after 10 years. If you look around, it's true. One of the reasons for this is that they don't take the time to listen to advisors.

Even Billy Graham, one of the greatest servants of God the world has ever seen, used to often call people up for advice. He would even call me when I was just a young, upstart evangelist! One time when he was going to go to the Vatican, he called me up and said, "Luis, I think I should go see the pope, but how do you think the Hispanics will react? Will it bring trouble?" He wasn't thinking of himself—there was a lot of persecution in Columbia at the time, and he wanted to make sure he didn't add to the trouble. As a Hispanic myself, he valued my input and advice.

I said, "Mr. Graham, I think it would be a great blessing even if some people criticize you, because if you have a foot in the door, God could use you to ease up the believers' persecution."

Billy Graham was the one who had opened doors for me as an evangelist. He was my mentor, yet here he was calling me for advice. After our conversation, I thought to myself, *When was the last time I called someone to ask for advice?* Scripture says that with many advisors, we succeed.

Another time, Billy Graham called me up and said, "Luis, what can I do for you?"

I wanted to say, "Give me a million bucks," but I had the prudence to say, "Please speak well of me." And he did.

One day, I thanked him for getting me the opportunity to preach in some place. He said, "Luis, I can only open the door for you, but you have to walk through it."

That's what the Luis Palau Association is now doing—opening doors for other evangelists. But to walk through the door, evangelists must have integrity, respect and holiness. People should be able to look at their lives and see a holy servant of God.

Proverbs 15:10 says, "He who hates correction will die." I have seen so many young evangelists who had so much potential—who had a tremendous gift from the Holy Spirit—fall away. If you and I don't live responsibly, we will never be as fruitful as we can be, and we may not be fruitful at all.

I once knew an evangelist who had a tremendous gift. Something about him drew people to him, and he could preach the gospel well. I was willing to be his crusade director, but when I did a crusade for him in Latin America in the 1960s, he never said "thank you." He never gave credit. He just acted like, "Hey, this is my thing. The rest of you are nobodies." When I recognized his attitude, I thought, *I'm not going to stake my life with this guy. He's going to mess up one of these days.* He didn't accept correction. Evangelists are notorious for messing up and giving the gospel a bad name.

This man had a gift of evangelism that was astonishing. I would sit there watching him, thinking, *If only I could be like this guy.* But he loved money too much. We found out only by a chance conversation with a friend that he died a few years ago. Nobody knew where he had been or what he had done at the end of his life. He lost 30 years of ministry. While we kept going with evangelism and crusades, this guy just disappeared.

Seek advice—it can keep you from making so many mistakes.

Avoid Temptation

After great victories, there are great temptations. The man who discipled me when I was young devoted an incredible amount of time to me. For three years, we met several times a week and spent two or three hours studying the Bible and praying. He would loan books to me and teach me straight from God's Word.

One of the things he taught me that I have never forgotten was about avoiding temptation. Scripture states that when David fell into immorality and murder, he was about 42. Nowadays, we would say he had a midlife crisis. My mentor warned me, "When you get to that age, be very careful. Basically, you become bored with your wife. You've been married about 20 years by then; you've had three or four babies. She's tired of sex, she's going through the change, and that's when you get tempted to look around." This is what David was going through. Even the best of us are tempted—even when we know what we are supposed to do and when we should be careful.

Another big temptation is to become careless and bored. It is so easy to become careless in your walk with God—and even cynical. We must keep our relationship with God fresh by spending daily time in His Word. Not just studying up for a big message, but one-on-one reflection and communion with the living God.

Finally, the love of money is another temptation that has destroyed too many evangelists. Of course, we need money to live and do our work. But there's a difference between *needing* money and *loving* money. Greed will destroy you.

Saint Clement of Alexandria said, "Wealth is like a viper, which is harmless if a man knows how to take hold of it; but if he does not, it will entwine around his hand and bite him." Naturally, we need money, and there's nothing wrong in welcoming it when the Lord sends it our way. Praise His name for it all—we need it to spread the good news around the world. But we shouldn't covet money for personal pleasure.

What a fine and delicate line some cross when they transfer funds from their ministry for unnecessary personal appropriation. Sensitivity from the Lord must mark our every move regarding money, or else we will "grieve the Holy Spirit of God" (Eph. 4:30) and lose His power for service.

We also face the risk of using money to impose our will over that of Christian brothers who might, in the Spirit, disagree with us. "You are witnesses," said Paul, "and so is God, of how holy, righteous and blameless we were among you who believed" (1 Thess. 2:10).

HAVE TENACITY

If you're going to go down in history as a servant of God who did great things, you have to have tenacity. Paul writes to Timothy,

"Continue in what you have learned and become convinced of" (2 Tim. 3:14). Don't give up. The forces that would try to stop you are endless. If you don't have tenacity, you will disappear from the scene in less than 10 years. Even if the numbers drop, keep on evangelizing.

No Team, No Dream

My friend Dr. Robnett told me this phrase, "No team, no dream," some time ago, and I really believe it. Jesus had a team. The apostle Paul had a team. And they were quality teams, though not necessarily high-class teams. We often say the disciples were just fishermen, but in those days, being a fisherman with a fleet of boats was a big deal. Acts points out that they were unschooled, but they had been with Jesus.

Of course, not every evangelist wants to have a team, and I honor and respect those who travel alone without a team. I find such evangelists amazing—that is a lonely job and must be a special guidance from the Lord.

However, if you wish to form a team, remember Psalm 37:4: "Delight yourself in the LORD and he will give you the desires of your heart." God will bring the right people to you.

Your spouse is your number one team member. Your children, when they grow up, become your number two group on the team. You should never force your children into evangelism, but what an honor to have your sons and daughters grow up to serve at your side!

Beyond your family, trust God to build the perfect team for you. When you ask God for a team, you should spend lots of time alone with Him. Jesus spent all night in prayer when He selected the Twelve and asked them to join His team, and even then He had a crook. Jesus' treasurer, Judas, was a thief and a traitor. So don't panic if one of your team members fails you.

As an evangelist, you are fighting a battle for souls, and you want team members who recognize this battle. You don't want any cynics on your team. Our bodies give out, but souls last for eternity. You need team members who are willing to battle.

You also want team members who have the missionary spirit, are willing to take less than "honorable" pay (at least in the early stages), and are willing to give their lives for Jesus, for the team, and even for you. As John 15:13 says, "Greater love has no one than this, that he lay down his life for his friends." I hope they feel that way about you and that you feel that way about them.

You cannot afford to have a team member who does not have a teachable spirit. Each person on your team has to accept your leadership. They don't have to agree with you all the time, but they have to accept you as a leader.

Another characteristic to look for is a servant attitude. When considering new people, I often measure how far they're going to go not only in our organization, but also in the kingdom of God. I particularly keep an eye on younger guys. I leave my suitcase by the open trunk of a car to see if the young man puts it in or walks by and thinks, *Put your suitcase in the car yourself, old man.* Anybody who hires people watches these things. Does this person really go out of his or her way, or does the person hide when you show up? You want people with servant attitudes.

Paul always traveled with team members. They were his blessing and protection. I praise God for my loyal team members constantly. Our ministry would be paralyzed without them.

As you organize your team, realize that you need people, but that you also need a purpose. Put your purpose in writing. Have a strategy. Know how you're going to get things done. Do you need to use the radio and other media? How are you going to get attention?

Once you have a purpose, you need goals—specific, measurable things you can do. First, write down your goals prayerfully. As an evangelist, you cannot afford to have unrealistic goals. Write down things that are reasonable and serious. These should not be just meaningless thoughts on a random piece of paper; they should be achievable objectives. If you can put Bible verses next to each goal, even better. Then write down the desires of your heart. Is it to have a certain number of campaigns a year? To preach to a certain number of people? This is serious stuff between you and God.

Your goals should be specific. Don't say, "I'd like to have all the money necessary to do my job." That is not enough. Say, "I need $800,000 a year," and put it before the Lord. Keep it confidential until the Lord gives you permission to share it, and then, as He gives you freedom, share it with people you trust. You will need other people to help you meet your goal, but don't put it in your newsletter only to later realize God isn't blessing that goal!

When you have about 10 goals, put them in order of importance—beginning with the most achievable. Every day, review them and pray about them. Watch to see what little steps you take each day to advance that well-crafted goal.

KEEP A GODLY INDEPENDENCE

While remaining deeply dependent on the indwelling Christ, we also need to keep a godly independence from other human beings. About 30 years ago in Latin America, there was a tremendous evangelistic movement. Evangelists were doing campaigns just like Billy Graham, and many of us evangelists wanted to join them.

One reason why Next Generation Alliance is not under the Palau umbrella is because of what I learned from that time. These evangelists were doing great things for God. But one of the great dangers when God uses you to do something big is pride. Suddenly, you think, *I am a man of God,* or, *I have a handle on the Kingdom.* That's why we have popes and cardinals and archbishops and deans and priests and denominations—everybody wants to be in charge of someone or something.

As an evangelist, you have to be careful. People love to come between you and God. There are many bitter old evangelists today who were stymied by powerful people and organizations that tried to throw up roadblocks in their way.

I was in Bogotá, Columbia, when one of the leaders of this evangelistic movement came up to me and said, "We have decided we are going to have an organization of evangelists, and we will all decide who goes where." He wanted to divide up the cities so that each evangelist spoke in a certain number each year.

I said, "I don't think so. I think evangelists should have the freedom to be led by the Holy Spirit."

Then he said, "If you don't join this organization, you'll be dead in three years." Well, that organization is the one that disappeared. Most people have never even heard of it.

These evangelists were great people, but they let the big things they were doing for God go to their heads. It can happen. That's why you should have a godly independence while also accepting counsel. If you're not humble, the Lord will crush you. So be humble, but keep a godly independence.

One day, Billy Graham said to me, "Luis, be very careful with big donors, because they want to run your life. It's better to have thousands of little donors who love you than to have a few big guys who want to tell you what to do."

The Lord made us to support each other, but unfortunately too many people let prestige get to their heads. Be careful not to let those kinds of people sway your ministry from its true purpose.

GO IN POWER

Paul wrote, "For God did not give us a spirit of timidity, but a spirit of power, of love and of self-discipline" (2 Tim. 1:7). The Lord Himself promised, "You will receive power when the Holy Spirit comes on you" (Acts 1:8). Power! Authority! Holiness!

A successful evangelistic ministry is built on more than just financial strength and a large team. Our personal holiness and that of our team members is of great importance. When we devote ourselves to God, He will bless us tremendously. Be careful to avoid the things that have brought down so many evangelists. Make a commitment now to seek Him first—and He will make everything else fall into place.

May God make you an awesome weapon for Him around the world in this generation!

CHAPTER 10

THE BALANCING ACT

MAINTAINING AN EVANGELISTIC MINISTRY

TIMOTHY ROBNETT

Some years ago, my wife and I toured a house that seemed more like a rambling collection of rooms than a place that one would want to call a home. The family that lived there had occupied the home for more than 30 years. As a need arose, they added on a room—an extra bedroom, a game room, a room to accommodate square dancing, a sunroom—and on it went. Yes, the family lived there. Yes, you could call it a house. But, oh, it certainly could have been designed and built more suitably.

Many work at evangelistic ministry in a similar fashion. As the need arises, they do something. Yet the Bible has outlined many key principles that liberate and empower God's children to minister the gospel more effectively than a hit-or-miss philosophy.

The evangelist equips Christians for evangelistic ministry by teaching, modeling and leading according to biblical principles. Seven principles stand out to me. These principles are like the foundation and frame of a house. A solid foundation and strong frame make for a secure and long-lasting structure, and when we as evangelists teach these principles, believers experience a new level of fruitfulness in evangelistic ministry. I'd like to assume that all evangelists, men and women, are exercising their calling by equipping the Church with these dynamic principles.

WORSHIP

Jesus taught that the Father is actively seeking worshipers (see John 4). When the members of the Church, individually and collectively, focus their lives on the worship of God in praise and obedience, they are dynamically empowered. A unique manifestation of God's Spirit comes when believers gather in Jesus' name to worship Father, Son and Holy Spirit.

As the first Church gathered for teaching, fellowship, breaking of bread, praising God and enjoying the favor of all people, the Lord added daily to those who were being saved. Evangelism was their way of life. Sharing the life of the risen Savior was their food. Their words and behavior mirrored the will of God, resulting in many coming to believe in Christ and live as they did. Today, as congregations gather to lift up the name of Jesus in songs of praise and adoration, people are drawn into the presence of God. Churches that experience the immanence of God through Spirit-directed worship impact those outside of Christ through the work of the Holy Spirit.

The psalmist said, "Taste and see that the LORD is good; blessed is the man who takes refuge in him" (Ps. 34:8). Dynamic worship has an evangelistic impact. Worship centered in Christ draws attention to the only One who can satisfy the soul. Evangelism in the context of the Church in Spirit-directed worship brings power to the good news. One needs to ask then, How are we doing as worshipers of Jesus Christ? Who is our focus of worship? Are we lifting up God? Are we cognitively and emotionally connecting with our Father? Is our worship about performance or performers? Does music style and instrument selection dominate the focus of worship? Or is worship about the God who is full of grace and truth?

As an evangelist, you need to establish personal worship as a pattern for life. Whether you call this discipline of the spiritual life your devotional life, your quiet time or your personal altar, a faithful and fruitful life of preaching the good news comes only out of listening to the Lord in personal time with Him. Luis Palau's leadership of a growing ministry flows from his time with the Lord, and it is evident to all that he consistently is a man in the Word and on his knees.

An evangelistic ministry also gains energy and power from the worship aspects of presenting the good news. Greg Laurie's Harvest Crusades have modeled for years the power of the Church in praise and worship. There, those without Christ experience the joy of worship as they hear and see the Church in worship. This is a powerful prelude to the presentation of the good news.

The festival style of evangelism used by the Luis Palau Association embraces a more contemporary and focused understanding of not only the power of music to reach the hearts of people—particularly the younger generations—but also the need in evangelism to guide people into an engagement with God with their minds, hearts and will. Worship invites people to respond to a loving and awesome God with heart and soul.

The Holy Spirit

Before the dark hours of the crucifixion, Jesus focused His attention on teaching the disciples about the coming and working of the Holy Spirit. He assured them that the Comforter was coming to be with them and live in them. Jesus challenged them with the thought that they would do greater works because He was going to the Father and the Holy Spirit was coming to minister through them to the world. The world that hated Jesus will hate us, but the Holy Spirit in and through us is greater than the opposition we face.

This second major principle of evangelistic ministry can be overlooked or exaggerated. Evangelists, in their personal life and public ministry, need to embrace and rely on the working of the Holy Spirit. For many evangelists, the realization of the working of the Holy Spirit in and through them is shared as a growth experience. Many serve for years before they fully embrace the empowerment of the One sent from heaven to guide and work through the Church to reach a lost and dying world.

After His resurrection, Jesus commanded His disciples to stay in Jerusalem until the Holy Spirit came upon them so that they would be empowered for evangelistic ministry. It is the fullness of the Holy Spirit that prepares any and all believers for harvest work. The Holy Spirit directs and empowers the words of the witnessing Christian. The illuminating power of the Holy Spirit chooses our words and gives insight to the lost person.

As the Holy Spirit inspired the authors of Scripture, so, in a similar way, He directs the words of those who are witnesses for Christ. Also, the Holy Spirit convicts the world through the life and words of the Church. Therefore, no evangelism can occur apart from the Holy Spirit. Believers are to be filled by the Holy Spirit for effective evangelistic ministry. Every evangelist needs to understand and experience the filling of the Spirit of Jesus for effective evangelistic ministry. Only in complete reliance on Him does one become active and effective in evangelistic ministry (see John 15—16; Acts 1:8; Eph. 5:18-20).

Where does the teaching of the working of the Holy Spirit come in your ministry? Dr. Bill Bright, through the ministry of Campus Crusade for Christ, taught hundreds of thousands of believers how to be filled by the Holy Spirit. This was a revolutionary principle that set many believers free from a legalistic form of evangelism. It allowed them to experience the joy of seeing God work through them in presenting the good news and of seeing people respond by faith to God's invitation to open their hearts to Christ. Each evangelist has been sent the Spirit to indwell and empower him or her for ministry.

FRUIT

A third principle for long-term evangelistic ministry emphasizes that the fruit of abiding in Christ will bring lasting fruit (see John 15:16). This refers to at least two things: first, the ongoing work of the Holy Spirit in drawing people to Himself through the life and witness of the Church; and second, the Holy Spirit maturing people in their walk with God through the Church's faithfulness and wisdom in discipling new believers.

I believe "fruit that remains" refers to people who come into the Kingdom and continue on in the faith, thus continuing in an abiding relationship with Christ. Those who exhibit an abiding relationship with Jesus Christ understand that being a Christian is not just an emotional experience, joining an organization or conducting themselves in a certain way, but that it involves allowing Christ to invade and control every dimension of their lives.

Disciples who want to become like Christ need models of Christlikeness. To bear fruit that lasts, each believer must focus on a long-term relationship with Christ. Disciples must begin with a decision for Christ, but they only continue on the journey of life following Christ if they abide in His Word. Evangelism is connected with discipleship making. Fruit that does not last has no root in Christ. Therefore, evangelism must focus on Christ, His Word and a long-term relationship with His Church (see John 15:1-12).

How is your evangelistic ministry equipping the Church to have practical ways of introducing people to a daily walk with God? Typically, you need a curriculum, Bible study, discipler or small group to nurture new believers. This takes planning as well as preparing the leaders and the course of study. A systematic approach that is relationally based has proven effective in hundreds of churches. What is your plan and program to stimulate the churches in this highly needed area?

UNITY

Jesus' prayer before His work on the cross, as expounded in John 17, focuses on a fourth principle: unity. We hear the deep longings of Christ for His Church, and at the center of Jesus' concerns is the unity of the Church. Jesus prays that the Church will be one even as He and the Father are one. Evangelism that does not flow from unity and that does not lead to unity of the Body of Christ cannot fulfill the will of Jesus. Evangelists can be those unifying persons who call the Church to partnership, cooperation and supportive ministry.

Unity brings focus in purpose and work. When people in the Church share a common purpose, a positive and productive energy flows in and through their relationships. When the Church works together in cooperative evangelistic efforts, relationships among Christians are strengthened, new ministries are often formed, people are brought into the Kingdom, churches are planted, and a God consciousness often comes over the city.

Often, this cooperative effort begins with united times of prayer. Prayer frequently leads to reconciliation in the Body of Christ. Believers get right with one another and with God, and when there is forgiveness, they begin to affirm one another and focus on God's agenda rather than on their own agenda. When the Body of Christ works together to fulfill the purpose of Christ's mission, whole cities and nations can be renewed, and the Church can increase in size and impact. Jesus said, "For the Son of Man came to seek and to save what was lost" (Luke 19:10).

What is your plan as an evangelist to unify the Church for the purposes of honoring Christ? Time and again, I have seen the beauty of the Body of Christ working together to reach the lost for Christ. There is no unity quite like the unity evangelism brings. When the Church is focused on the passion of Christ in reaching those not yet embraced by His saving grace, a special and compelling energy fills the Church. This positive power pulls people together like nothing else.

Evangelist, God's call upon your life is for you and your ministry to unite the Church, not to divide it. But how can you help bring this unity? First, believe what Jesus prayed in John 17. Second, call the Church to unity around Christ and the good news, not some other agenda. Third, make prayer a foundational principle for all your ministries, both private and public. Fourth, listen to the Spirit through the stories of those you are working with. Honor the Church by believing that the Spirit is speaking today. You may have to develop some flexibility, but the outcome will be a united Church that is dynamically sharing the good news as never before in communities all across the world.

INTENTIONALITY

The fifth principle of evangelistic ministry is intentionality. Without an intentional purpose and plan, people typically do not get around to living the priorities they profess. "Intentionality" is a keyword in evangelism. Just as farmers plan each year to sow seed, cultivate that seed, and then reap a harvest from the same seed, so evangelists can inspire the Church to intentional seasons of evangelistic harvest.

Jesus compared the winning of the lost to reaping a harvest. Just as farmers can expect a harvest, believers can expect God to bring the lost into His family through the work of those who sow the good news of Jesus, cultivate relationships with intentional acts of love and mercy, and expect God to draw the lost into His family.

The evangelist is strategic in keeping the Church on task. Yes, evangelism is a task of reaching people through meaningful friendships, but those friendships need to be intentional. We need to love the lost. The Church needs to consistently initiate relationships with those outside the family of God. This takes prayer, focus, alertness, compassion, energy and faith. In addition, it may take days, months or years of cultivation before people turn to Christ. So we must keep at it.

Evangelists need to remind and encourage the Church to be faithful in cultivating relationships, for we never know when the day of a person's salvation will come. For some, the day arrives during childhood; for others, when they are teens; for still others, when they are young adults, young parents, or in the middle years of adulthood—and the Lord waits for some at the very last day of their earthly journey. But whatever time a person comes to Christ, the Church needs to be alert and ready, waiting for and wanting their loved ones and friends to embrace the most beautiful person in the universe, Jesus Christ. Evangelist, your role is to inspire the Church to keep at it. Don't give up. Be faithful, for we do not know when those we have waited for will come to Christ.

PRAYER

The sixth principle, prayer, remains one of the most available means of ministry. Prayer, though often unexplainable, is irreplaceable in the working of God, and He uses it in amazing and unusual ways. Prayer gives us a connection with divine power to all ministries, and through it we have communion with God, and God with us.

Prayer allows the believer to engage with God through personal dialogue. But prayer is also a weapon of spiritual warfare. It activates spiritual resources against the enemy, Satan, and opens the lost to the good news of Jesus. It protects and inspires. It is a ministry of the gospel (see Eph. 6:19-20; Col. 4:1-6; 1 Tim. 2:1-4).

Ephesians 6:19-20 expounds the truth that the children of God need prayer to overcome their fears of evangelistic ministry. Paul, the apostle, asked the believers to pray that God would give him boldness in sharing the gospel. Why would the great apostle need boldness? By this request, Paul revealed his own fears and his need for God's power through the prayer of others to overcome those fears. If the apostle Paul had fears, I imagine we all do when it comes to speaking clearly about the good news of Jesus to others.

Why do we have fears in our witnessing for Jesus? Because we still live in our fallen human flesh and struggle continually with the fears and failures of our carnal minds and timid souls. This is a condition of all people not living under the power of the Holy Spirit—a condition that finds a remedy only in the power of God released in us. When we pray and others pray for us, an unnatural and appropriate boldness is released in and through our lives. Prayer is irreplaceable in the ministry of evangelism.

Fears may also come because of our ignorance as to what to say or how to respond to unbelievers. Prayer once again enlightens our minds and brings us confidence in God. Many times, our enlightenment comes in the heat of a discussion or in the perplexity of a situation far beyond our control. Luis Palau gave a great on-the-spot response to a Chinese government official in November 2005 while recording a video project entitled "A Friendly Dialogue Between an Atheist and a Christian." Mr. Zhao, a skilled scientist and admitted atheist, said to Luis, "I can only believe in what I can test in a laboratory." Luis responded to Mr. Zhao, "You are the laboratory of God." This spontaneous yet highly appropriate response demonstrates the inspiring work of the Holy Spirit in and through us. The discussion took on a decidedly personal and powerful nature when Luis used this metaphor of the person being God's laboratory for engaging God and spiritual life.

The apostle Paul also realized that evangelistic opportunities could not be just a creation of human ingenuity. Rather, divine appointments for the gospel needed to be made by God Himself. God, the author of salvation, orchestrates the application of the good news to each person's life. Colossians 4:3-5 emphasizes the reality that God is acting in human history to bring openings for the gospel to be preached. Often, the opportunity for preaching the gospel only needs eyes that will see and a mouth that will speak (see Rom. 11:8). Prayer creates opportunities by removing the scales from the eyes of the believer and calluses from the believer's heart. Only with divine power does this transformation take place.

Paul, though held up as a model Christian, struggled with the opposition that made him blind and hard to the ministry of reconciliation. But prayer overcomes what we cannot manufacture. When we pray, we are being reconstructed into God's image and likeness. We behave as He would. Evangelistic opportunities are birthed when Christians bow to pray and rise to embrace those open doors.

URGENCY

The seventh principle comes from Paul's second letter to the Thessalonians, which contains these words: "Pray for us that the message of the Lord may spread rapidly and be honored . . . and pray that we may be delivered from wicked and evil men" (3:1-2).

Paul's early years in Europe were characterized by urgency and persecution. This virgin soil for the gospel contained some responsive hearts, but most were indifferent, skeptical or full of hate. Paul and his traveling team faced opposition on a regular basis, so he requested that the young believers in Thessalonica pray that the good news of Jesus would make a quick impact on the culture. This request for responsiveness was no doubt also accompanied by Paul's knowledge of the great need of the people who were struggling through their existence with no hope of eternal life.

Evangelists have an urgent mission. Every day, 165,000 people die worldwide, and every soul who has never heard the good news faces an eternity without Christ. Millions upon millions face each day without the knowledge of Christ and the salvation He can bring into every moment of their lives. There is a need for God to empower the Church for quick and honorable action.

This "honorable action" could refer to the receptivity of the gospel—that it is received and believed, that people do not scorn the good news but seriously consider it, and that they then respond to this special message from God by opening their hearts to Christ. But it also refers to the way in which the good news is presented, which would then speak to how the Church presents the gospel. Is the gospel presented in a loving and practical manner? Is the gospel presented in words and deeds? Is the good news spoken to the lost with respect and with deep conviction? Paul says we should pray for this atmosphere in evangelistic ministry.

Paul, with a note of reality, also asked for prayers that the messengers of the good news be protected from evil men. There are

opponents to the good news. There are many people who have much
to lose when families, cities or nations are confronted with the
gospel. Those who make their living from evil means and those who
govern from selfish motives are just some of the people who will suf-
fer when others abandon their lifestyles for the sake of the gospel.

The evil one holds many in darkness, fear and hatred. Although
they need the gospel, often their first reaction to the good news of
Jesus is hostility, not joy. The movie *The End of the Spear* records the
sad yet redemptive story of the Akka Indians in Ecuador who, out of
fear and confusion, murdered five young missionaries. The end of
the story reveals that the power of the gospel—in this case through
the love of the murdered missionaries' families—can redeem a lost
people. Yet the pain and suffering by those who first brought the
message should not be ignored or denied. Prayer is essential for the
Church to stand against the evil and wicked people we face each day.

Your evangelistic ministry will be built on something. What
foundation are you laying for a lifetime of evangelistic ministry?
These principles guarantee that you will find that God is far more
committed to your effectiveness than anyone else you know. God
believes in His mission of reaching the lost. You are part of His sin-
gular strategy of using the Church as the communicator of His
good news. Your time is now. God has provided. Go for it!

CONCLUSION

Imagine what would happen if every man, woman and child in your area heard the gospel of Jesus Christ clearly proclaimed and committed their lives to Him this year.

Why, every newspaper around the world would take notice! Every radio station would report "the greatest revival of all time." Every television newscast would discuss the dramatic reformation taking place.

But our work still would not be finished. What about the children? What about the future immigrants? And what about the more than 3 billion people in the world who have never heard a clear presentation of the gospel?

Statistics overwhelm us. So let's think about the specific individuals we have met who have never committed their lives to Christ. Who comes to mind? Now let's think about the crowds we see in cities, at train stations, in streets—everywhere. How do you feel when you think about them?

Scripture tells us that when Jesus saw the crowds, "he had compassion on them, because they were harassed and helpless, like sheep without a shepherd" (Matt. 9:36). We need to ask God to move our hearts with the same compassion that moves His heart.

The greatest dangers we face as Christians are cynicism and detachment. *So, more than 3 billion people don't know Christ. That's too bad.* We must not forget the actual people—including those we know and love—behind that number who live "without hope and without God in the world" (Eph. 2:12).

The Lord pointed out the urgency of our task by reminding His disciples, "The harvest is plentiful but the workers are few" (Matt. 9:37). We must sense the urgency of our time. How long must people wait before they hear the gospel? How many more generations must pass before some parts of the world hear the message of Christ for the first time?

It's exciting to see that there is a tremendous harvest in most of the Third World today. Several nations in Latin America and Africa could become 51 percent Christian within 15 years, and God is at work in Asia as well. Right now, the doors are open as perhaps never before in history. Mass communication has made it possible to reach even closed nations with the message of life. All of this is before us now, but it could pass in a short time.

Our task is urgent. That's why Christ commanded His disciples, "Ask the Lord of the harvest, therefore, to send out workers into his harvest field" (Matt. 9:38). Our Bibles end that chapter of Matthew right there, but don't stop reading! In the next five verses, the Lord gave His disciples authority and sent them out. The Twelve became an answer to their own prayer!

In order to finish the task, we must have the authority of God that comes from a holy life. Paul told Timothy, "God did not give us a spirit of timidity, but a spirit of power, of love and of self-discipline" (2 Tim. 1:7). I like to think of this as holy boldness.

The unfinished task of winning the world to Christ is enormous. Are you willing to gain a compassion for the unsaved and a sense of urgency in reaching them for Christ? Are you available to God to serve with holy boldness as a worker in His harvest? Let's press on to finish the task set before us.

WHEN ALL IS SAID AND DONE

A 10-year-old girl made the following observation: "Heaven is a nice place to go, but nobody's in a hurry to get there." And, you know, she's almost right.

Why is it that many Christians aren't excited about going to heaven and seeing the Lord? Maybe it's because, when all is said and done, unless their lives change, they will have little or nothing to show for their lives.

Christians in our society have opted for the good life. They go to church, read their Bibles, serve on church committees, tithe and don't do a single thing that will count for eternity. Why? Because they refuse to do the one thing that God has called them to do: love Him with all their heart and soul and strength (see Mark 12:30).

If we love God with every fiber of our being, we will long to be with Him. We will say with the apostle Paul, "For to me, to live is Christ and to die is gain" (Phil. 1:21). Paul wasn't afraid to die, because he knew he had a glorious future awaiting him in heaven. And the exciting thing for us won't be the streets of gold, but that "God is with men" (Rev. 21:3).

In addition, if we love God with all our heart and soul and strength, we will do what He calls us to do. Love and obedience cannot be separated. The Lord Jesus Christ made this clear to His disciples when He said, "If you love me, you will obey what I command" (John 14:15).

What are the consequences of not heeding God's call on our lives to serve Him as He intended? I found out one snowy January while preaching at a church in Schenectady, New York.

Before the meeting started, a rather distinguished-looking gentleman with a cane entered the sanctuary, walked to the front of the church, introduced himself and asked to speak with me after the service. We arranged to meet at the home of the family with whom I was staying.

In the car on the way to their house, my hosts told me about the gentleman with the cane. "Luis," they said, "you need to know that this gentleman is one of the most distinguished ophthalmologists in the country. His textbooks are studied in many of the major universities. He's been away from the Lord since we were in university together, but something has been on his heart during the last few weeks."

At the house, my hosts excused themselves so the doctor and I could talk privately for a few minutes.

"Young man," he said, "I have a question to ask you, and based on the answer you give me, I'm going to make a big decision. I'm an ophthalmologist. I've made a lot of money. I'm well respected. Most people think I'm a success. But my daughter has no interest in God, and my son is going to hell because I've never shared the gospel with him. For years, I've questioned how I've spent my entire adult life. Is that success?"

Then he explained further. "When I was in university, some 42 years ago, a missionary by the name of John R. Mott came and spoke about the need in the Middle East for ophthalmologists to help treat eye diseases, and I felt the call of God. When he gave the invitation, I made a commitment to go and serve Jesus Christ on the mission field. I made a commitment to use my medical skills for God's glory.

"But when graduation came, I married, and my friends and relatives began to warn me about the dangers of living in the Middle East, the sacrifices a missionary must make, and about foolishly wasting my education. They said, 'Don't do it.' The pride of life got a hold of me, and I never did go to the mission field. Instead, I started my own practice here in the States."

Then he added, "I want you to know, I haven't had one day of peace in 42 years. Now I'm retired, and I've asked my wife to go with me to Afghanistan so we can finish our last days serving the Lord in mission work. I've said, 'Let's at least obey God at the end of our lives.' But she doesn't want to go. So tell me, shall I go or shall I stay?"

In typical Latin fashion, I put my arm around him and said, "Brother, I believe you should go."

He began to cry. "Thank you! I will go. God's been calling me for 42 years. This time no one is going to stop me."

Three months later, I phoned the family I had stayed with in Schenectady. "How is the doctor doing?" I asked.

"Haven't you heard?" they replied. "He's off to Afghanistan, and his wife went with him. He's coming back to the United States soon to collect medical supplies donated from some large companies to use over there. He's as excited as he can be."

The next winter, I had the privilege of returning to Schenectady. The doctor was there as well. His body had grown so weak that he couldn't even stand up anymore. But on the inside he was very much alive.

"Come here," he said. "Give me one of those Latin hugs." After I greeted him, he told me, "The next time I see you, I'm going to see you in the presence of the King!" A few weeks later, he went to be with the Lord.

What moved me about this doctor was the fact that he had no peace for 42 years because he rebelled against the Lord calling him to the mission field. When he looked back over his life, he realized that all his great accomplishments were worthless because he had not obeyed God's plan for his life.

What is our supreme responsibility as Christians on this side of heaven? To be a success? Yes, but a success in God's eyes. Henrietta Mears said, "Success is anything that is pleasing to Him." I agree. We please God when we commit ourselves wholeheartedly to doing whatever He calls us to do.

Someone once asked William Booth about the secret of his success. He thought for a moment and then started to cry. He said, "I will tell you the secret: God has all there was of me to have."

Does God have all there is of you to have? As the doctor from Schenectady discovered, it's never too late to follow God's will for your life, no matter how long you've neglected His call. It's never too late to please Him.

And what a beautiful thing it is when someone finally returns to the ways of God and is prepared to enter eternity victoriously.

Are you looking forward to heaven? Are you ready and eager to go? Imagine the Savior saying to you, "Well done, good and faithful servant! You have been faithful with a few things; I will put you in charge of many things. Come and share your master's happiness!" (Matt. 25:21).

When all is said and done, what will the Lord say to you?

APPENDIX

TIME LINES OF EVANGELISTS

Most mass evangelists do not become so overnight—it is a lifelong process. The following time lines provide a few examples of the road to growing an evangelistic ministry.

Luis Palau

Year	Event
1934	Born in Buenos Aires, Argentina, on November 27
1944	Father dies
1947	Confesses Jesus Christ as Savior at a summer camp led by a Saint Alban's teacher
1951	During a particularly tempting Carnival Week in Buenos Aires, decides to dedicate his life to serving Christ
1952	Given a trainee's position with the Bank of London in Buenos Aires; hears Billy Graham on radio for the first time; preaches first outdoor evangelistic meetings and has first radio ministry
1960	First involvement in a ministry combining evangelism and church planting; leaves Argentina for further education in the United States
1963	Ordained a Christian minister in Palo Alto, California
1964	Starts a gospel radio program, which develops into *Luis Palau Responde* and *Cruzada,* now heard daily by an estimated 22 million people in the Spanish-speaking world; begins writing ministry
1968-70	Begins concentrated ministry in Mexico; Mexico City crusade attracts 106,000 people, with 6,670 inquirers (those who publicly commit their lives to Jesus Christ); gains attention throughout Latin America

1974   First book, *Walk on Water, Pete,* published in English and Spanish

1976   Named president of OC International

1976-77 First Northern European ministry, with evangelistic meetings in West Germany and Wales; crusade in Rosario, Argentina, solidifies Palau Team's church growth emphasis; dozens of new churches are planted

1978   The Luis Palau Evangelistic Association (LPEA) incorporates as an independent organization with headquarters in Portland, Oregon; first motion picture, *God Has no Grandchildren.*

1982   On November 28, an estimated 700,000 people attend crusade in Guatemala City, Guatemala, the largest single audience in Palau Team history

1983-84 Begins two-phase Mission to London, the Palau Association's longest crusade to date, with attendance reaching 518,000; *Commonwealth '84* radio broadcasts from London crusade reach 50 English-speaking nations worldwide

1984-86 Three-continent-wide radio broadcasts: *Commonwealth '84, Continente '85;* and *ASIA '86*

1989   Holds first open-evangelistic meetings in the modern era in Hungary and the Soviet Union

1990   Invited by Romania's newly formed Evangelical Alliance to preach in Oradea, Bucharest and Timisoara; an estimated 46,100 people make decisions for Christ

1991   Returns to Romania for crusades in five cities; 31 per-
         cent of the 125,900 people who hear the gospel make
         decisions for Jesus Christ

1997+   Receives repeated invitations to the White House; minis-
         ters to President Clinton and President Bush

1998   Seventy evangelists attend the first Next Generation
         Alliance Evangelists Conference at LPEA's international
         headquarters

1999   The Palau ministry reinvents itself by launching the fes-
         tival model of evangelism; "Great Music! Good News!"
         Festival sets new attendance records at Tom McCall
         Waterfront Park in downtown Portland, Oregon
         (crowds of 55,000 and 85,000)

2003   Beachfest Ft. Lauderdale becomes the largest U.S. festi-
         val ever staged by the ministry, attracting more than
         300,000 to south Florida during Spring Break; Livin It
         skateboard ministry is launched

2005   Festivals held in Madrid, Spain, and Washington, D.C.

2006   *Live It Live LA* released

TIMOTHY ROBNETT

Year	Event
1950	Born in Coalinga, California
1957	Conversion to Christ at a church evangelistic campaign
1970	Responds to call to serve Christ; ministers with youth outreach choir in California
1970-72	Speaks regularly to youth groups; begins sports evangelism with Campus Crusade for Christ and Fellowship of Christian Athletes
1977	Becomes Pastor of Youth and Family at West Park Baptist Church
1978	Ordained at West Park Baptist Church in Bakersfield, California
1979-90	Pastor of Palm Springs Baptist Church; conducts pastoral leadership for Conservative Baptists Association of Southern California
1985-86	Hosts Bob Cryder evangelistic ministries; starts Evangelism Explosion Ministry at Palm Springs Baptist Church
1986	Begins doctorate studies at Fuller Seminary
1989-90	Leads pastors' committee for the Luis Palau Crusade in Palm Springs, California—in-depth exposure to mass evangelism in a local community

1990   Becomes international crusade director for the Luis
Palau Association, working in Asia, the Caribbean,
United States and northern Europe

1996   Begins teaching evangelism at Multnomah Bible
Seminary

2000+   Becomes director of Next Generation Alliance;
coordinates evangelistic outreaches in Asia,
Europe and Africa

KEITH COOK

Year	Event
1957	Born in Dyersburg, Tennessee
1972	Receives Christ as Savior while watching a gospel film at the Springfield Baptist Church in Springfield, Tennessee
1973	Called into evangelistic ministry; preaches first sermon at Springfield Baptist Church
1973-86	Holds U.S. Revival and Youth Crusades
1974	Starts Keith Cook Evangelistic Association
1975	Launches radio ministry
1977	Ordained at First Baptist Church in Trezevant, Tennessee
1980	First international project (Korea); called into world evangelism
1983	Networks with international ministries

1990 Launches GoTeams (short-term evangelism projects)

1992 Launches GoCamps (training camps on missions/ evangelism)

1998 Speaks to more than 200,000 people worldwide (6,248 decisions to follow Christ are made)

2000 Speaks to more than 295,000 people worldwide

2002 Speaks to 350,000 in Brazil, Jamaica, Costa Rica, Haiti and the United States

2005 Focuses on festival model and On the Go Neighborhood Outreach methods

JOSE ZAYAS

<u>Year</u> <u>Event</u>
1972 Born in New York City

1979 Responds to Christ through 700 Club television program

1987 Preaches first message (age 15)

1994 Meets Luis Palau

1995 Graduates with degree in Church Ministries/Evangelism

1996 Starts teaching evangelism training classes for Luis Palau Association

1998 Preaches at event in England

2000   Becomes partner evangelist with the Luis Palau
Association

2000   Forms Jose Zayas Evangelism International (JZEI)

2001   Hosts outreaches in the United States, South Africa,
Uganda and England; speaks with Billy Graham in
Romania

2003   More than 35,000 attend outreaches in East Europe tour

2004   JZEI reaches more than 85,000 with events in the
United States, China and Uganda

2005   Partners with Dare2Share; speaks to students in evangelism

2006   Prepares for new model of evangelism: THRIVE festivals

2006   Board changes ministry name to Starting Point Outreach

STEVE WINGFIELD

Year	Event
1947	Born near Lynchburg, Virginia

1970   Receives Christ as Savior at a crusade

1974   Graduates from Eastern Mennonite University in
Harrisonburg, Virginia

1981-83 Works with evangelist Clyde Dupin and as a crusade
director for Dr. Myron Augsburger

1983-85   Attends Trinity Evangelical Divinity School in Deerfield, Illinois

1985   Forms Wingfield Ministries, Inc. (now Steve Wingfield Evangelistic Association)

1988   Wingfield Ministries annual budget at $100,000, with four staff members

1989   Preaches in Romania during the fall of communism

1992-97   Ministry expands from four to eight staff members

1998   Partners with Next Generation Alliance

1999   Hosts five crusades in one year

2000   Conducts the *2000 Encounter* event in Canton, Ohio; uses major multimedia for the first time

2002   Ministry grows to 11 full-time staff members

2004   Begins using the festival model of evangelism; holds three to five festivals each year from this point forward

2005   Hosts Proclamation Evangelism Network conference at *Springfest '05* in Harrisonburg, Virginia; leads a Hurricane Katrina recovery effort that raises more than $1 million in aid for Long Beach, Mississippi

2006   Ministry annual budget reaches $1.3 million, with 13 staff members

For a good framework for understanding the significant lessons of life's journey, refer to *The Making of a Leader* by J. Robert Clinton (Colorado Springs, CO: NavPress Publishing Group, 1988).

ABOUT THE AUTHORS

Dr. Luis Palau stands out in this generation as a truly international Christian spokesman and leader. He's a third-generation transplanted European who grew up in the province of Buenos Aires, Argentina, and then chose to become an American citizen after completing graduate work at Multnomah Biblical Seminary in Portland, Oregon.

Equally at ease in English and Spanish, Luis Palau commands audiences' attention wherever he goes. His solidly biblical, practical messages hit home in the minds and hearts of listeners.

Up to 400,000 people now turn out for his popular weekend evangelistic festivals in key cities across the United States.

"Sometimes it seems I have been preaching all my life," the world-renowned evangelist says. "Actually, although I started preaching in Argentina as a teenager, it really wasn't until I was in my 30s that God opened the door for me to pursue full-time mass evangelism. And now that I'm in my 70s, He's opening up even bigger doors."

Those bigger open doors include publishing three evangelistic books for Doubleday, one of the largest secular publishers in New York; starting *Reaching Your World with Luis Palau,* a daily radio program airing on more than 850 affiliates; and launching Next Generation Alliance, a ministry that actively assists younger evangelists. "Billy Graham and others took the time to build into my life years ago. Thanks to their mentoring, I was spared a lot of unnecessary grief and dead ends," Luis says. "I'm now committed to coming alongside other younger, gifted evangelists."

Luis Palau often jokes that he plans to serve the Lord until he's 92. Why 92? "Well," he says, "when I was young, I read a biography of George Mueller, who had such a dynamic ministry to orphans in Bristol, England, during the nineteenth century. I lost my own dad when I was 10 years old, so Mueller's story really made an impression on me. Especially the part that he kept right on serving until he died at age 92. In fact, two Sundays before he died, he was in the pulpit preaching the Word. Why can't I aim for the same?"

What does Luis look forward to over the next 20 years?

"First, my dream is to see the Muslim world open up to the gospel.

"Second, I'd love to have an opportunity to minister in every nation. We're already using literature, radio, television and the Internet to reach tens of millions of people in 120 nations. But nothing can replace face-to-face ministry.

"Third, I'm praying for the Lord to raise up a new generation of godly evangelists who can saturate whole cities with the life-changing message of Jesus Christ.

"Fourth, I want to be faithful to the end."

Luis has a great passion for evangelizing the world and for helping the next generation of godly evangelists spread the voice of God worldwide.

Since 1990, **Dr. Timothy Robnett** has served God's call to lift high the banner of biblical evangelism. Today, he trains and encourages hundreds of emerging evangelists as the director of Next Generation Alliance, a ministry of the Luis Palau Association dedicated to training up the next generation of godly evangelists.

Before moving into full-time evangelistic ministry, Dr. Robnett spent 18 years in the local church as a youth pastor, associate pastor and senior pastor. In 1990, he joined the Luis Palau Evangelistic Association as International Crusade Director, and he has coordinated evangelistic festivals and crusades in the United States and in Asia, the Caribbean, Europe and the South Pacific.

In 1996, Dr. Robnett was invited to join the faculty of Multnomah Biblical Seminary as Associate Professor of Pastoral Ministry and Internship Director. He has taught a wide range of courses, including Evangelism for the 21st Century, Workshop on Evangelistic Ministries, Ministry Management and Development, and Leadership Growth and Development.

Dr. Robnett has published articles in a variety of evangelism and ministry journals, including *Preaching,* and he served as theological reviewer for the *Starting Point Study Bible* published by Zondervan, a 2003 Gold Medallion Award finalist.

After graduating from Stanford University in Palo Alto, California, with a bachelor's degree in sociology, Dr. Robnett received his master of divinity degree from Western Conservative Baptist Seminary in Portland, Oregon. He earned his doctor of ministry degree at Fuller Theological Seminary in Pasadena, California.

Dr. Robnett and his wife, Sharon, and their two children, son, Joel, and his wife, Kate, and daughter, Karen, live near the international headquarters of the Luis Palau Evangelistic Association in Portland, Oregon.

Through preaching, teaching, training and publishing, Dr. Robnett's desire is for the evangelists of the next generation to be fully prepared to bring the good news of Jesus Christ to every corner of the earth.

About Next Generation Alliance

History of NGA

"After more than 35 years of mass evangelism," says Luis Palau, "I believe the task of proclaiming the gospel of Jesus Christ is more urgent than ever. Hundreds of millions have never heard about the cross of Christ and His saving work. In obedience to the Great Commission, we need to do everything we can to reach them with the good news of forgiveness and eternal life."

"Let's work together!" That's the rallying cry that gave birth to Next Generation Alliance in 1998. Next Generation Alliance, working together with and sharing the resources God has entrusted to the Luis Palau Evangelistic Association, is multiplying the impact of many evangelists throughout the world.

Together, they hope to flood America and the world with the gospel of Jesus Christ.

The Vision for NGA

"Hold high the banner of biblical evangelism . . . raise up a new generation of godly leaders . . . so that the Church's commitment to evangelism will never die," says Timothy Robnett, director of Next Generation Alliance.

Encouraging evangelists is a major objective of the Luis Palau Evangelistic Association. Sadly, there are too many evangelists around the world who are deeply discouraged and ready to quit.

The Great Commission that God has given the Church requires each of us to keep at it with greater cooperation and effectiveness. To this end, we're expanding Next Generation Alliance to make it an even more useful resource for every evangelist and to help all evangelists see the fulfillment of their dreams of monumental impact for God's glory.

What Is NGA's Mission?

We desire to fulfill the Great Commission in our generation by re-establishing the strategic role of the evangelist by working through, with and for the Church worldwide.

What Does NGA Do?

- Identifies and affirms evangelists
- Provides resources for mentoring, training and equipping evangelists
- Positions evangelists to preach the gospel in strategic locations and to unreached people groups
- Teaches and trains local churches on the work of evangelists
- Partners with other groups through collaborative evangelistic ministry events

How Does NGA Minister?

- Through a network of independent evangelists: partner, network, emerging and member
- By providing evangelists with practical service opportunities such as collaborative evangelistic festivals
- Through training opportunities:
  - NGA Conferences: in Portland and also international venues
  - Collaborative Trainings: such as the PEN conference
  - Seminars: designed for specific needs held at the Portland headquarters of the Luis Palau Association
  - Extend the Impact: gatherings at Luis Palau Association festivals to connect NGA evangelists with opportunities for ministry in specific geographical regions
  - With the Academic Community: partnerships with Multnomah Biblical Seminary, Michigan Theological Seminary, Gordon-Conwell Theological Seminary and the Academy for Evangelism in Theological Education

Organizational Structure of NGA

- A ministry of the Luis Palau Association
- Director serves as a cabinet member of the Association
- NGA staff report to the Director
- The Director and staff serve the NGA evangelists by networking, resourcing and training
- NGA members are encouraged to mentor other evangelists

Selected Bibliography

Abraham, Kumar. *Rediscovering the Spiritual Gift of the Evangelist and Its Implications for the Church Today*. Dissertation presented to the Asia Graduate School of Theology, Manila, Philippines, March 2006.

Allen, Roland. *The Ministry of the Spirit*. Grand Rapids, MI: Wm. B. Eerdmans Publishing Company, 1960.

——. *Missionary Methods: St. Paul's or Ours?* Grand Rapids, MI: Wm. B. Eerdmans Publishing Company, 1962.

——. *Missionary Principles*. Grand Rapids, MI: Wm. B. Eerdmans Publishing Company, 1964.

——. *The Spontaneous Expansion of the Church*. Grand Rapids, MI: Wm. B. Eerdmans Publishing Company, 1962.

Allison, Lon, and Mark Anderson. *Going Public with the Gospel*. Downers Grove, IL: InterVarsity Press, 2004.

Barna, George. *Evangelism That Works: How to Reach Changing Generations with the Unchanging Gospel*. Ventura, CA: Regal Books, 1995.

Bauer, Scott. *Crusade Evangelism*. Unpublished dissertation studying the impact of a Luis Palau Crusade on the growth of The Church on the Way, 1994.

Bergin, G. Fred, comp. *Autobiography of George Muller*, 3rd ed. London: J. Nisbet and Company, 1914.

Berkley, James D., ed. *Leadership Handbooks of Practical Theology. Vol. 2, Outreach and Care*. Grand Rapids, MI: Baker Book House, 1994.

Bonar, Andrew A. *Memoir and Remains of Robert Murray M'Cheyne.* Edinburgh, Scotland: The Banner of Truth Trust, 1973. First published 1844.

Bonar, Horatius. *Authentic Records of Revival.* Wheaton, IL: Richard Owen Roberts Publishers, 1980. First published 1860 by James Nisbet and Company, London.

Bready, J. Wesley. *England: Before and After Wesley.* London: Hodder and Stoughton, n.d.

Brown, Elijah P. *The Real Billy Sunday.* Dayton, OH: Otterbein Press, 1914.

Burns, James. *The Laws of Revival.* Minneapolis, MN: World Wide Publications, 1993.

Careaga, Andrew. *eMinistry.* Grand Rapids, MI: Kregel Publications, 2001.

Chafer, Lewis Sperry. *True Evangelism.* Grand Rapids, MI: Zondervan Publishing House, 1967. First published 1919.

Chandler, Russell. *Racing Toward 2001.* Grand Rapids, MI: Zondervan Publishing House, 1992.

Coleman, Robert E. *The Master Plan of Evangelism.* Old Tappan, NJ: Fleming H. Revell Co., 1993.

Curtis, Richard K. *They Called Him Mister Moody.* Grand Rapids, MI: Wm. B. Eerdmans Publishing Company, 1967.

Dallimore, Arnold. *George Whitefield.* London: The Banner of Truth Trust, 1970 (vol. 1) and 1979 (vol. 2). Published by Cornerstone Publishers in the United States.

Dorsett, Lyle W. *Billy Sunday and the Redemption of Urban America.* Grand Rapids, MI: Wm. B. Eerdmans Publishing Company, 1991.

Douglas, J. D., ed. *The Calling of an Evangelist.* Minneapolis, MN: World Wide Publications, 1987.

——. ed. *Let the Earth Hear His Voice.* Minneapolis, MN: World Wide Publications, 1975.

Drummond, Lewis. *Reaching Generation Next: Effective Evangelism in Today's Culture.* Wynwood, 2002.

Edman, V. Raymond. *Finney Lives On.* Minneapolis, MN: Bethany House Publishers, 1971.

Ellis, James J. *Charles Haddon Spurgeon.* London: James Nisbet and Company, n.d.

Ellis, William T. *"Billy" Sunday: The Man and His Message.* Philadelphia: John C. Winston Company, 1914. Later revised and published in 1959 by Moody Press.

Fay, William, and Linda E. Shepherd. *Share Jesus Without Fear.* Nashville, TN: Broadman and Holman Publishers, 1999.

Ferm, Robert O. *Cooperative Evangelism.* Grand Rapids, MI: Zondervan Publishing House, 1958.

——. *Billy Graham: Do the Conversions Last?* With Caroline M. Whiting. Minneapolis, MN: World Wide Publications, 1988.

Findlay, James F., Jr. *Dwight L. Moody: American Evangelist, 1837-1899.* Chicago: University of Chicago Press, 1969.

Finney, Charles G. *An Autobiography*. Old Tappan, NJ: Fleming H. Revell Company, n.d. First published as *Memoirs of Charles G. Finney*, 1876.

Fitt, Arthur Percy. *The Shorter Life of D. L. Moody*. Chicago: Moody Press, n.d. First published as *Life of D.L. Moody* by W. R. Moody and A. P. Fitt, London: Morgan and Scott, 1900.

Ford, Leighton. *The Christian Persuader*. New York: Harper and Row, Publishers, 1966.

Fountain, Jeff. *The Final Frontier*. Eastbourne, England: Kingsway Publications, 1987.

Getz, Gene. *The Measure of Spiritual Maturity*. Richardson, TX: Grace Products Corporation, 1993. Eleven-part video series and workbook.

Gibbs, Alfred P. *The Preacher and His Preaching*. Kansas City, MI: Walterick Publishers, n.d.

——. *A Primer on Preaching*. Fort Dodge, IA: Walterick Printing Company, n.d.

Graham, Billy. *A Biblical Standard for Evangelists*. Minneapolis, MN: World Wide Publications, 1984.

——. *Revival in Our Time: The Story of the Billy Graham Evangelistic Crusades*. Wheaton, IL: Van Kampen Press, 1950.

——, et al. *Choose Ye This Day*. Minneapolis, MN: World Wide Publications, 1989.

Grasso, Domenico. *Proclaiming God's Message.* Notre Dame, IN: University of Notre Dame Press, 1965.

Green, Michael. *Evangelism in the Early Church.* Grand Rapids, MI: Wm. B. Eerdmans Publishing Company, 1970.

Hardman, Keith J. *Seasons of Refreshing.* Grand Rapids, MI: Baker Book House, 1995.

—. *The Spiritual Awakeners.* Chicago: Moody Press, 1983.

Henry, Carl F. H., and W. Stanley Mooneyham. *One Race, One Gospel, One Task.* 2 vols. Minneapolis, MN: World Wide Publications, 1967. A compendium of the World Congress on Evangelism, Berlin 1966.

High, Stanley. *Billy Graham.* New York: McGraw-Hill Book Company, 1956.

Hoffman, Warren L. *The Secret of the Harvest: Mobilizing for Team Evangelism.* Evangel Publishing, 1996.

Holton, Susan, and David L. Jones. *Spirit Aflame.* Grand Rapids, MI: Baker Book House, 1985.

Howard, David M., ed. *Declare His Glory.* Downers Grove, IL: InterVarsity Press, 1977.

Hughes, Philip Edgcumbe. *Theology of the English Reformers.* London: Hodder and Stoughton, 1965.

Huston, Sterling W. *Crusade Evangelism and the Local Church.* Minneapolis, MN: World Wide Publications, 1984.

Johnston, Arthur. *The Battle for World Evangelism.* Wheaton, IL: Tyndale House Publishers, 1978.

Johnstone, Patrick. *Operation World,* 5th ed. Grand Rapids, MI: Zondervan Publishing House, 1993.

Kennedy, D. James. *Evangelism Explosion,* 4th ed. Wheaton, IL: Tyndale House Publishers, 2002.

Latourette, Kenneth Scott. *A History of the Expansion of Christianity.* 7 vols. Grand Rapids, MI: Zondervan Publishing House, 1970. First published 1937-1945 by Harper and Row Publishers.

Lazell, David. *Gipsy Smith: From the Forest I Came.* Chicago: Moody Press, 1973.

Lyall, Leslie T. *John Sung: Flame for God in the Far East.* Rev. ed. Chicago: Moody Press, 1964.

Macfarlan, D. *The Revivals of the Eighteenth Century.* Wheaton, IL: Richard Owen Roberts Publishers, 1980. First published 1847 by Johnston and Hunter, Edinburgh, Scotland.

Martin, William. *A Prophet with Honor: The Billy Graham Story.* New York: William Morrow and Company, 1991.

McGavran, Donald Anderson, ed. *Church Growth and Christian Mission.* New York: Harper and Row, Publishers, 1965.

Miller, Basil. *Charles G. Finney.* Minneapolis, MN: Bethany House Publishers, 1966.

Mitchell, Curtis. *Billy Graham: Saint or Sinner.* Old Tappan, NJ: Fleming H. Revell Company, 1979.

——. *God in the Garden*. Garden City, NY: Doubleday and Company, 1957.

——. *The Making of a Crusader*. Philadelphia: Chilton Books, 1966.

Moody, William R. *The Life of D. L. Moody*. New York: Fleming H. Revell Company, 1900.

Orr, J. Edwin. *The Second Evangelical Awakening*. Rev. ed. London: Marshall, Morgan and Scott, 1964.

Packer, J. I. *Evangelism and the Sovereignty of God*. London: InterVarsity Fellowship, 1961.

Palau, Luis, with David Sanford. *Calling America and the Nations to Christ*. Nashville, TN: Thomas Nelson Publishers, 1994.

——. *Healthy Habits for Spiritual Growth*. Grand Rapids, MI: Discovery House Publishers, 1994.

——. *Heart for the World*. Manila, Philippines: OMF Publishers, 1989. Published for the Lausanne II in Manila Congress on World Evangelization.

——. *The Only Hope for America*. With Mike Umlandt. Wheaton, IL: Crossway, 1996.

——. *Renewing Your Spiritual Passion*. Edmonton, Alberta, Canada: Crown Video, 1992. Three-part video series.

——. *Say Yes: How to Renew Your Spiritual Passion*. Grand Rapids, MI: Discovery House Publishers, 1994.

——. *What Is a Real Christian?* Portland, OR: Multnomah Press, 1985. Published in 32 languages worldwide.

Parker, Percy Livingstone. *The Journal of John Wesley.* Chicago: Moody Press, n.d.

Peters, George W. *Saturation Evangelism.* Grand Rapids, MI: Zondervan Publishing House, 1970.

Pierson, A. T. *George Müller of Bristol.* London: Nisbet and Company, n.d.

Pollock, John. *Billy Graham.* New York: McGraw-Hill Book Company, 1966.

——. *Billy Graham: Evangelist to the World.* San Francisco: Harper and Row, Publishers, 1979.

——. *George Whitefield and the Great Awakening.* Garden City, NY: Doubleday and Company, 1972.

——. *Moody.* Grand Rapids, MI: Zondervan Publishing House. Published in the United Kingdom as *Moody Without Sankey.* London: Hodder and Stoughton, 1963.

——. *Wilberforce.* New York: St. Martin's Press, 1977.

Quist, Allen and Timothy Robnett. *Spirit-Driven Church.* Colorado Springs, CO: Cook Communications, 2006.

Robertson, Darrel M. *The Chicago Revival, 1876.* Metuchen, NJ: Scarecrow Press, 1989.

Robinson, Haddon. *Biblical Preaching.* Grand Rapids, MI: Baker Book House, 1980.

Schaff, Philip. *History of the Christian Church.* 8 vols. Grand Rapids, MI: Wm. B. Eerdmans Publishing Company, n.d. First published in 1866.

Scharpff, Paulus. *History of Evangelism.* Translated from 1964 German edition. Grand Rapids, MI: Wm. B. Eerdmans Publishing Company, 1966.

Schubert, William E. *I Remember John Sung.* Singapore: Far Eastern Bible College Press, 1976.

Smith, Oswald J. *The Passion for Souls.* London: Marshall, Morgan and Scott, 1950.

——. *The Revival We Need.* London: Marshall, Morgan and Scott, 1940.

Spurgeon, C. H. *C. H. Spurgeon: Autobiography.* Vol. 2. Edinburgh, Scotland: The Banner of Truth Trust, 1973. First published 1897-1900 as the last two of four volumes.

——. *The Soul-Winner: How to Lead Sinners to the Saviour.* Grand Rapids, MI: Wm. B. Eerdmans Publishing Company, 1963.

——. *Spurgeon—The Early Years.* London: The Banner of Truth Trust, 1967. First published 1897-1900 as the first two of four volumes.

Stott, John R. W. *The Cross of Christ.* Leicester, England: InterVarsity Press, 1986.

——. *Preacher's Portrait.* Grand Rapids, MI: Wm. B. Eerdmans Publishing Company, 1961.

Streett, R. Alan. *The Effective Invitation.* Old Tappan, NJ: Fleming H. Revell Company, 1984.

Strobel, Lee. *Inside the Mind of Unchurched Harry and Mary.* Grand Rapids, MI: Zondervan Publishing House, 1993.

Strober, Gerald S. *Graham: A Day in Billy's Life*. Garden City, NY: Doubleday and Company, 1976.

Telford, John. *The Life of John Wesley*. New York: Eaton and Mains, n.d.

Tracy, Joseph. *The Great Awakening*. Edinburgh, Scotland: The Banner of Truth Trust, 1976. First published 1842.

Triton, A. N. *Whose World*. London: InterVarsity Press, 1970.

Tucker, Ruth A. *From Jerusalem to Irian Jaya: A Biographical History of Christian Missions*. Grand Rapids, MI: Zondervan Publishing House, 1983.

Tuttle, Robert G. *John Wesley: His Life and Theology*. Grand Rapids, MI: Zondervan Publishing House, 1978.

Weakley, Clare George, Jr. *The Nature of Revival*. Minneapolis, MN: Bethany House Publishers, 1987.

Whitefield, George. *George Whitefield's Journals*. Edinburgh, Scotland: The Banner of Truth Trust, 1960. First published 1738-1747.

——. *Letters of George Whitefield*. Edinburgh, Scotland: The Banner of Truth Trust, 1976. First published 1771 as *The Works of George Whitefield*.

Wood, A. Skevington. *The Burning Heart: John Wesley, Evangelist*. Exeter, England: Paternoster Press, 1967. Published in the United States by Bethany House Publishers, 1978.

Woodbridge, John, gen. ed. *More than Conquerors: Portraits of Believers from All Walks of Life*. Chicago: Moody Press, 1992.

Wright, Linda Raney. *Christianity's Crisis in Evangelism.* Gresham, OR: Vision House Publishing, 1995.

Luis Palau Association

Reaching the World Through
INNOVATIVE EVANGELISM

www.palau.org

HIGH DEFINITION LIFE

livin it

LUIS PALAU

Innovative

LUIS PALA

Luis Palau Association | Post Office Box 50 | Portland, OR 97207 |
503.614.1500 | info@palau.org

GET INVOLVED
each More People for Christ

LUIS PALAU'S
NEXT GENERATION ALLIANCE®

www.NGATeam.com

nnect with other evangelists | >

Ministry outreach opportunities | >

gn up for upcoming events | >   Forums | >

"Ask Luis" Area | >   Evangelism Blog | >

Download MP3 training sessions | >

xt Generation Alliance | Post Office Box 50 | Portland, OR 97207

nga@palau.org

Let Your Light Shine

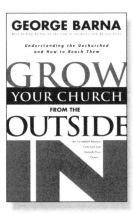

Grow Your Church from the Outside In
George Barna
Understanding the Unchurched and How to Reach Them
ISBN 08307.30753

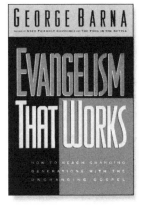

Evangelism That Works
George Barna
How to Reach Changing Generations with the Unchanging Gospel
Paperback • ISBN 08307.17765

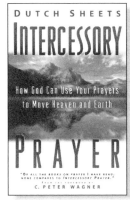

Intercessory Prayer
Dutch Sheets
How God Can Use Your Prayers to Move Heaven and Earth
ISBN 08307.19008

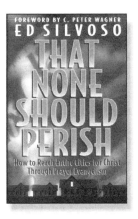

That None Should Perish
Ed Silvoso
How To Reach Entire Cities For Christ Through Prayer Evangelism
ISBN 08307.16904

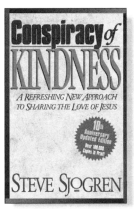

Conspiracy of Kindness
Steve Sjogren
A Refreshing New Approach to Sharing the Love of Jesus
ISBN 08307.34074

Prayer Evangelism
Ed Silvoso
How to Change the Spiritual Climate Over Your Home, Neighborhood and City
ISBN 08307.23978

Available at Bookstores Everywhere!
Visit **www.regalbooks.com** to join **Regal's FREE e-newsletter.** You'll get useful **excerpts from our newest releases** and **special access to online chats with your favorite authors.** Sign up today!

 **Regal**
God's Word for Your World™
www.regalbooks.com